ROYAL COPLEY

MIKE
SCHNEIDER

Schiffer Publishing Ltd

77 Lower Valley Road, Atglen, PA 19310

Copyright © 1995 by Mike Schneider

Library of Congress-in-Publication Data

Schneider, Mike.
Royal Copley: identification and price guide / Mike Schneider
p.   cm.
Includes bibliographical references (p.   )
ISBN: 0-88740-739-0
1. Royal Copley--Collectors and collecting--United States--
Catalogs. 2. Pottery figurines--Ohio--Sebring--Catalogs. I. Title.
NK4340.R78S36   1995
738'.09771'39--dc20   94-41367
CIP

Printed in Hong Kong

We are interested in hearing from authors with
book ideas on related topics.

Published by Schiffer Publishing Ltd.
77 Lower Valley Road
Atglen, PA 19310
Please write for a free catalog.
This book may be purchased from the publisher.
Please include $2.95 for postage.
Try your bookstore first.

These personalized *Teddy Bear Banks* may have been made by one of the John or Jane Does to whom the book is dedicated, perhaps as gifts to their children or other relatives. Note the black paws and ears on the brown one, which are unusual. Each bank is 7-7/8 inches high, neither is marked. For more *Teddy Bear Banks* see page 21. Estimated value: brown $50, white $65. *Osborne Collection.*

DEDICATION

This book is dedicated to the John and Jane Does of America's once thriving pottery industry--the slip mixers, mold makers, ballers-in, sagger carriers, decorators, common laborers and all the others, who, predominately, worked for low wages in uncomfortable and health threatening conditions to produce the once common items we collect and treasure today. While those of us who write about mid-twentieth century American pottery often tend to emphasize owners and designers, we should always try to remember that it was the nameless workers on the floor who actually made the beautiful pieces we illustrate.

This lamp, bearing the Royal Copley seal, turned up near Sebring, Ohio, the location of the Spaulding Chnia Company. While one may speculate about its purpose the most likely possibility is that it was used at various trade shows as part of the company's exhibit. *Carson Collection.*

Fish Vases do not come along very often, especially with gold decoration, especially in gray. Each vase is 6 inches high, neither is marked. A third *Fish Vase* is shown on page 84. Estimated value: yellow with gold $60, gray $50. *Osborne Collection.*

ACKNOWLEDGMENTS

Most of the Royal Copley, Royal Windsor and Spaulding pieces displayed in this book belong to Linley and Joyce Carson, who over the years have put together one of America's most complete collections of the Spaulding China Company's numerous wares. Cindy and I spent three days photographing it. During that time the warmth and friendliness of both our hosts in general, and the scrumptious cooking of Joyce in particular, made it seem more like we were on an epicurean vacation with longtime friends than actually working with acquaintances we had known but a short while. We were introduced to Linley and Joyce by Linley's brother and sister-in-law, Floyd and Betty Carson, wonderful friends who have always gone out of their way to allow me to photograph their things for my books.

Linley Carson introduced us to another avid collector, Rachel Osborne, who also graciously permitted us to photograph some pieces we could not find elsewhere.

Another journeyman collector, Charlie Gold, did the same thing. Actually, either Rachel's or Charlie's collection could have formed the foundation of the book had we not met Linley and Joyce first.

As usual, and as I have come to depend upon, Cindy attended each photo session and diligently recorded information about each piece that appears in the book.

Others who contributed in various ways were editor Douglas Congdon-Martin, designer Sue Taylor, pot-and-pan mogul Fred Fatula, and collectors Doris Dyer, Allen and Michelle Naylor, and Ted and Lee Parent.

The piece on the left is 7-5/8 inches high, the piece on the right 7-7/8 inches. They are the *Chinese Boy and Girl with Big Hat Planter/Wallpockets.* They are unmarked, have two runners. These planter/wallpockets in several other color combinations can be seen on page 101. Estimated value: $25 each. *Carson Collection.*

CONTENTS

True figural items such this *Rocking Deer Planter*, 6 inches high and unmarked, will be found in Section II Figural Ware, Chapter 4 Animals. Since the book is arranged in alphabetical order, deer figurals appear closer to the beginning of the chapter than, say, sheep (rams and lambs), which show up farther back. Estimated value: $45. *Osborne Collection.*

The *Black Floral Leaf and Stem Vase* with gold decoration is an example of a nonfigural piece having a raised decoration, which would place it in Section III Nonfigural Ware, Chapter 8 Three-dimensional Motif. The vase is 3-1/4 inches high, and carries a Shaffer gold stamp. Estimated value: $20. *Osborne Collection.*

══════ A NOTE ABOUT NAMES ══════

Names of pieces that appear in *italics* and begin with capital letters are the names that were used by Leslie C. and Marjorie A. Wolfe in their books, *Royal Copley, Plus Royal Windsor and Spaulding*, and *More About Royal Copley, Plus Royal Windsor and Spaulding*, which were first published during the 1980s. Over the years these names have been readily accepted by collectors and have become a part of the jargon within the hobby.

Names that appear in regular type and do not begin with capitals, for the most part, are associated with pieces that had not yet been discovered or verified at the time the Wolfes authored their books, and thus did not appear in them. In some cases they are applied to pieces that were included in the Wolfes' books but were not assigned names.

When not referring to specific pieces, marks or paper labels the terms Royal Copley, Copley, and Spaulding have been used interchangeably throughout the text.

Section III Nonfigural Ware, Chapter 9 Non-three-dimensional Motif contains examples such as these rather plain vases. Heights are 4-3/8 inches on the left, 3-7/8 inches on the right. Both have USA impressed in their bottoms. Estimated value: $5 each. *Carson Collection.*

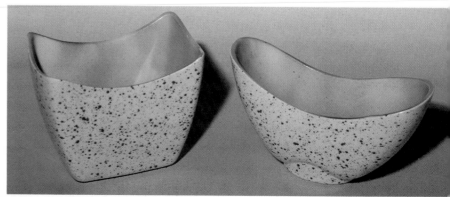

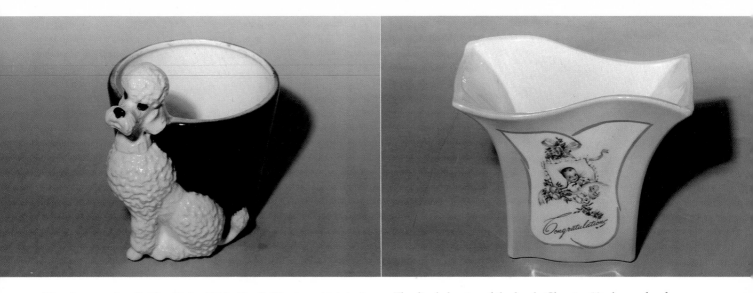

Here is a tough call. The *Sitting White Poodle Planter*, which is 6-3/8 inches high and unmarked, could probably qualify for nonfigural ware with three-dimensional motif since the dog is sitting by a plain flower pot instead of a figural object such as a suitcase or a mailbox. However, because the poodle itself is so obviously figural it will be displayed in Chapter 4 which shows figural animals. This may be a little confusing at first, but once you become familiar with the book it should cause little problem. Estimated value: $15. *Carson Collection.*

The final chapter of the book, Chapter 10, shows decalware, which would include examples such as this baby vase. The piece stands 6 inches high. It is not marked. Estimated value: $25. *Osborne Collection.*

═══ HOW TO USE THIS BOOK ═══

For your convenience, this book has been set up in three sections.

Section I Spaulding and Its Wares, contains introductory chapters covering history, marks, and values. Sections II and III, which carry most of the pictures are the real meat of the book so I will explain them in a little more detail.

Section II Figural Ware, as the title implies, shows only true figural pieces such as the *Rocking Deer Planter* on page 6. It does not picture things like the black *Floral Leaf and Stem Vase*, which would be described as nonfigural ware with a three-dimensional motif, and found in Chapter 8. Section II is divided into four chapters in alphabetical order whose subjects are animals, birds, miscellaneous, and people. The contents of the chapters themselves are also in alphabetical order. For example, you will find that cats appear before deer, deer before dogs, dogs before elephants, etc.

Section III Nonfigural Ware has three chapters. Their titles are Three-dimensional Motif, Non-three-dimensional Motif, and Decal Ware. Examples of each are shown below. Chapter 8 Three-dimensional Motif is arranged alphabetically, the other two are not.

With the book so arranged, and with the estimated values included with the captions, I hope this will provide you an easier to use reference than has been available in the past.

This is the *Tony Planter/Wallpocket,* named by the Wolfes for Tony Priolo the man who designed it. While you may find one or another of its features prominent on similar items by Shawnee, Hull, McCoy and other contemporaries of Spaulding, you will not find the exact combination of large size, intricate design, bold colors, precision airbrushing, planter-wallpocket adaptability and low cost on any of them. This is representative of the uniqueness that made Spaulding a viable pottery manufacturer in a highly competitive field. The *Tony Planter/Wallpocket* stands 8-3/4 inches high, is not marked but has three runners. This is the only color combination of which I am aware, but there may have been lunch hour pieces or special orders that were finished differently. Estimated value: $50. *Carson Collection.*

Although it existed only 15 years, the Spaulding China Company, like all successful pottery operations, changed, to a certain degree, American tastes in ceramics and interior decoration by offering new and slightly different products than its predecessors and contemporaries. This section covers the birth, life and death of Spaulding, and how to distinguish its slightly different products from those of other potteries. It also tells how those once commonplace and taken-for-granted items reemerged years later as collectibles, and explores the different avenues down which they may proceed in the future.

During the years that Spaulding was active, bird figurines were one of its most popular products. Like most of the pottery's output, they were marketed through five-and-ten-cent stores, yesteryear's embryonic retail outlets that eventually grew into today's giant discount stores. This picture shows the *Swallow with Extended Wings* from both sides. The figures are 7-1/4 inches high. They are not marked. The *Swallow with Extended Wings* is one of the rarer birds Spaulding produced. Check page 72 for a blue version. Estimated value: $45 each. *Carson Collection.*

CHAPTER 1
HISTORY

Spaulding China Company, the pottery that produced Royal Copley, Royal Windsor, and Spaulding, was owned by Irving Miller and Morris Feinberg, a pair of New York businessmen who operated the Miller Kitchen Clock Company. During the early days of the clock concern, Miller and Feinberg imported the ceramic clocks they sold. Sometime around 1930, however, they began purchasing clock works from the Ingraham Clock Company of Bristol, Connecticut, to fit into clock cases manufactured in Europe. While this arrangement apparently helped their bottom line, it left much to be desired due to the many months it took to get a new clock from the design tables to store shelves. And if the new clock sold well, large reorders stole more precious time, during which interest in the new item could dwindle as competitors introduced other designs to challenge it.

A subsidiary domestic pottery seemed the ideal solution to the problem. If they owned their own pottery, Miller and Feinberg could have immediate control over production schedules and quality, and potentially hold a tighter rein on costs, too. Delivery time on orders could be reduced from months to weeks. Their ceramic kitchen clocks would reach consumers while their interest was still piqued.

Toward that end, sometime in the mid-1930s, Feinberg ventured to Sebring, Ohio, long a pottery manufacturing center, and contracted with a small pottery to manufacture clock cases for them. Sometime later, most likely 1939

or 1940, the pair bought the pottery outright in order to more fully exercise the control they desired.

And that very well might have been the end of the story: Miller and Feinberg putting Connecticut clock works in Ohio clock cases and living happily ever after. No Royal Copley. No Royal Windsor. No Spaulding. But the unfairytale-like, volatile nature of the real world refused to allow it.

On December 7, 1941 the Japanese bombed Pearl Harbor. The next day the United States declared war on Japan, and brass, the essential material for making clock works, was diverted to the war effort and was unavailable to private industry. This cast Miller and Feinberg into the unenviable and capital draining position of owning a factory that could produce as many clock cases as they wanted, but being unable to get any works to put in them.

Fortunately, just as the supply of brass had dried up, so had the supply of imported ceramics that had long been a staple of five-and-ten-cent stores, yesteryear's smaller equivalents of today's larger discount stores. Miller and Feinberg saw the opening, shifted their emphasis and charged full speed ahead, the first kiln of Spaulding China artware and giftware pottery being fired in 1942. Spaulding's kilns kept on firing through 1957, and then continued even longer by proxy.

But before the Spaulding China Company existed as we know it, the pottery moved twice. First from its original small plant on East Ohio Street in Sebring to a building in Alliance formerly occupied by the Alliance Vitreous China Company. Sebring and Alliance are about five miles apart. The second move took Spaulding back to Sebring to still larger quarters that at one time had housed the Sebring Rubber Company. According to Jenny B. Derwich and Dr. Mary Latos, in *Dictionary Guide to United States Pottery and Porcelain--19th and 20th Century* (Jenstan, 1984), this last move was accomplished sometime in 1941. Although production of clock cases was still modest at that time, the later success of Royal Copley and the other lines eventually led to the operating floor being expanded to 58,000 square feet. The work force is said to have peaked at 200, give or take a few. When the company moved to this plant it installed a straight tunnel kiln and a decorating kiln. Sometime prior to 1948 increased demand for its wares led to the scrapping of the tunnel kiln in favor of a much more efficient continuous circular kiln. The decorating kiln was also dismantled, signalling an end to the manufacture of decal ware and gold decorated ware at the plant. Gold decorating was apparently contracted out, as evidenced by the many Shaffer marks found on Spaulding items. Decal decorating may have been contracted out, too.

The Spaulding China Company closed in 1957. However, according to the Wolfes, China Craft, a Sebring pottery owned by former Spaulding employee Ralph Brown, agreed to fulfill Spaulding's existing contractual obligations, which took approximately two years. With all due respect to the Wolfes, it seems more likely that along with agreeing to honor Spaulding's contracts China Craft purchased some or all of Spaulding's molds, as it continued using them for more than 15 years after the company's demise. Carrying things a step further, while China Craft may have lived up to Spaulding's standards during the two years it filled its existing orders, it apparently did not live up to them later when it made and marketed *Bending Head Mallard Duck Figurines*, and *Baby Bending and Erect Heads* to go with them, in colors so pale they looked anemic. (See Chapter 5 Birds page 56 for pictures and a more detailed explanation.) Consequently, some of the objects in this book, and in your collection, may not have been made by Spaulding but by China Craft during that initial two years, or possibly later. While further information may surface at some point in the future, at this time it is often impossible to differentiate between the two company's products.

After Spaulding closed in 1957 its orders were filled for a couple years by China Craft, a neighboring pottery owned by a former Spaulding employee. Pieces with a pebble glaze, such as this *Teddy Bear Bank*, originated during the China Craft period. Standing 5-1/2 inches high, this unmarked piece, along with its companion figurine on page 21, may have been made by China Craft exclusively. I am not aware of either of these bears, which hold the sucker horizontally, being found with a paper label, and the airbrushing on the figurine, is not consistant with other Copley bears. Estimated value: not determined. *Osborne Collection.*

Airbrushing was the password in the decorating department at Spaulding, as evidenced by this 8-inch high unmarked *Oriental Boy Figurine*. Note how each color varies from weak to strong, how one overlaps with another such as on the shirt cuff which includes both the flesh of the hand and the red of the shirt, and how the change from one color to another forms a murky transition instead of a clearly defined line, perhaps illustrated best by the brown spots on the shoes. More *Oriental Boy Figurines,* along with *Oriental Girl Figurines,* appear on page 100. Estimated value: $15 each. *Carson Collection.*

CHAPTER 2
IDENTIFICATION AND MARKS

Most of the output of the Spaulding China Company was not marked in any permanent manner. In other words, the company relied chiefly on paper labels to pass its name on to consumers. Today, 50-odd years and uncountable washings after the first labels were applied, the majority of them no longer exist. Be that as it may, paper labels are still the chief means of positive identification.

There is little doubt that after you collect Royal Copley awhile you will find pieces that appear to be Copley but are not marked, and are not shown in this book or any other. They will possess some or all of the identifying features shown and described below, and you will know in your heart they were made by Spaulding. But how can you be sure? The answer is that you can't until you, or someone else, find the piece with a paper label, or positively identify it through an old catalog sheet. Networking is great for this, collectors getting together in person, by letter, fax, telephone or computer, and comparing notes and pictures.

So what are the identifying features alluded to above? There are several of them. We will cover them one at a time.

Weight is one of the major ones. Spaulding China pieces were poured rather heavy. They are nearly always heavier than look-alike imports, sometimes heavier than similar domestic examples. After you lift a few hundred pieces of Copley your brain will subconsciously tell the

When finished in yellow the Wolfes referred to this bird as a *Canary,* when finished in blue a *Sparrow.* Either way it is a striking example of the rich strong colors Spaulding incorporated into its glazes. These figurines are 5-1/4 inches high. They are not marked. Estimated value: $25 each. *Carson Collection.*

This *Floral Leaf and Stem Vase* with gold decoration stands 8" high. It carries a Shaffer gold stamp, and like the majority of Spaulding's output, it has identifying runners on the bottom which are shown below. Estimated value $15.

The runners on the bottom of the *Floral Leaf and Stem Vase* above. Runners are ridges that were wiped dry while the glaze on the piece was still wet. Often called a dry foot, the runners prevented the pottery from being fused to the kiln during firing. While runners do not positively identify an item as Copley they can often provide the confirming evidence in cases where other characteristics lead you to believe it is Copley.

muscles in your arm exactly how heavy a given item ought to be when you are about to pick it up. If it rises much more quickly than you expected, there is good reason to believe it may not be Spaulding. Likewise, if your fingers slip on it because it was a lot heavier than you thought it would be, look on it with equal suspicion. But don't necessarily disregard it. I have seen some pieces with paper labels that for one reason or another were poured much lighter or heavier than normal. Perhaps a new employee. Perhaps an employee with a hangover. Maybe a rush order. For whatever reason it did happen occasionally.

Color helps a lot in the identification process. As you can see throughout the book, Copley used strong colors, rich colors, deep colors. Even its light colors were rich and strong. If a piece has glaze that appears faded or weak except in areas where one color overlaps another, it is probably not Copley.

Airbrushing. The company thrived on it. Look at any representative collection of Spaulding China and you will almost get the feeling there must have been a sign above the entrance to the factory, "All paint brushes must be checked at the door." With the exception of gold trim, pieces that have any handpainting that was applied with a paint brush are quite rare. The small, round, black eyes of the bird figurines and planters were probably done by hand. But considering their usually perfect roundness and identical size they were most likely done with an eye tool, which is best described as a device similar to a tapered toothpick with a small sphere at the end instead of a point; it is faster to use and much more accurate than the finest brush.

No paint. While many potteries used glaze and paint in combination, the only Spaulding piece I can think of that has paint on it is the *Barber Pole Razor Blade Receptacle* shown on page 80. Paint often chips. Paint often washes off. Paint deteriorates when exposed to extremes of temperature and humidity. Glaze is permanent. It often crazes but seldom falls off. If you do find an occasional Spaulding piece with paint on it, other than the *Barber Pole*, it's a fairly safe bet the paint was applied either after the piece left the factory, or by an employee who was making it to take home.

Many Spaulding items have **runners** on their bottoms. Other potteries did this, too. The runners could be wiped dry immediately after the liquid glaze was applied to the bottom, thereby giving the piece a "dry foot" to sit on when it was fired, which prevented it from being fused to the kiln. Like all of the other indicators, runners do not necessarily verify a piece as Spaulding, but they do lead you in that direction.

We should also take a moment to talk about Shawnee and American Bisque, the two potteries that are most often confused with Spaulding. The pictures shown below should eliminate 90 percent of the confusion. As you can see, Shawnee pottery, on the inside and bottom, is most often an off-white or cream color. Spaulding is generally pure white. Also, Shawnee is known for having used a dryfoot that often ringed the base. And American Bisque, while similar to Spaulding in nearly every other respect, used wedges instead of runners to attain a dryfoot. As far as is known, Spaulding never used wedges on the bottom of its pottery.

Now on to **marks**. A few Spaulding pieces were marked permanently with raised lettering, for instance, "Royal Copley," built into the mold. A more commonly used permanent mark was an inkstamp under the glaze. But the majority of Spaulding's output was not marked except by paper label. A cross section of both permanent marks and paper labels are shown on pages 13 through 16. (In some of the pictures colors are off due to incorrect exposure.)

You will note that with few exceptions the marks and labels say Royal Copley, Royal Windsor, or Spaulding. While these have generally been considered to be three separate lines, each targeted to a specific market such as dime stores or florists, it has become apparent over the years that the factory was not as particular about keeping them separate as was previously thought. Pieces that usually have Royal Copley paper labels show up with Royal Windsor paper labels, items in the Spaulding line sometimes appear with Copley labels, and so forth. While many collectors still consider them three separate lines, my observation is that a growing number of aficionados feel that the distinctions have become murky, and that it really makes no difference anyway as all Spaulding pottery is of similar quality regardless of which sticker is on it.

A pottery whose work ran parallel to Spaulding's was American Bisque, which made this puppy planter. Usually any doubt you have about an unknown American Bisque piece being a Spaulding piece will be removed once you pick it up and look at the bottom, which is shown below. *Courtesy of Allen and Michelle Naylor.*

American Bisque used what are commonly referred to as wedges on its pottery to provide a dry foot for firing. American Bisque wedges are generally rounded toward the outside of the piece, then come to a point toward the inside, such as the one shown here on the left.

This pig planter was made by Shawnee, a pottery whose style was similar to Spaulding's. One of the best ways to distinguish a Shawnee piece from a Spaulding piece is by the color of the inside and bottom, which as you can see, might best be described as cream or ivory. Uncolored areas on Spaulding products are generally pure white. *Courtesy of Allen and Michelle Naylor.*

Shawnee marks are different, too, usually but not always an impressed USA plus a number, or just the USA. (The mark area of this pig planter is actually the same cream color as the inside but is different in the picture due to a lighting error when the photo was shot.)

15

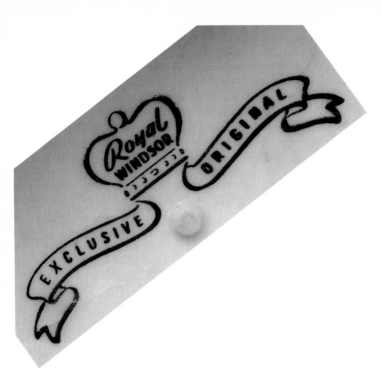

"BOOKS OF REMEMBERANCE"
by
ROYAL WINDSOR

DESIGN PATENTED

Being a figural this 9-1/2 inch high *Deer and Fawn Planter* with gold decoration is currently in demand and would be easy to sell if you decided to liquidate your collection. A marked piece, it has Royal Copley in raised letters on the bottom. More *Deer and Fawn Planters* can be seen on page 28. Estimated value: with gold $40, without gold $25. *Osborne Collection.*

CHAPTER 3
VALUES–YESTERDAY, TODAY AND TOMORROW

There was a time, and it wasn't that many years ago, when you could go to an estate auction and buy a cardboard box full of Royal Copley for $5. And in with it you might find a coffee can full of rusty nails, an ancient and dried out half gallon of paint, and anything else upon which the auctioneer failed to coax a bid. Those with foresight back then - 15 to 20 years ago - built some wonderful Copley collections for very little money. At that time a collector's main concern was that the can of nails and the paint can did not cause chips, and that people in the crowd would not make too many jokes about the fool who bought all that gaudy junk pottery.

But those days are gone. The baby boomers have come of age. A substantial number of them seek nostalgic satisfaction by spending their weekends at flea markets and antique shows in an effort to reacquire the material memories of their parent's and grandparent's homes of the 1950s and 1960s. Also, a sufficient amount of time has passed that Copley can now be characterized as belonging to the as yet unnamed period of mid-twentieth century ceramic design that succeeded Art Deco, preceded the flood of cheaper imports from Asia. As a result of these circumstances prices have skyrocketed. Today, if you were at an antique show buying the contents of the above mentioned cardboard box from that estate auction of yesteryear, you would likely have to pay anywhere from $5 or $6 to almost $100 for each piece.

A nonfigural, this *Double Spray Planter*, 4-1/2 inches high and unmarked, does not seem to kindle the same interest among collectors as the *Deer and Fawn Planter* above. Consequently, it not only sells for less, but would very likely take longer to unload if at some future point you should want to convert your collection to cash. A *Double Spray Planter* in chartreuse appears on page 121. Estimated value: $10. *Osborne Collection.*

For the most part the price structure of Copley is three-tiered. Figurals are the most expensive. Nonfigural items with three-dimensional motif make up the middle tier. Nonfigurals without three-dimensional motif occupy the bottom. There are exceptions, as there are to any general rule. But the simple truth is that collector interest runs higher for figurals than for nonfigurals. In a practical sense this means that the prices you see in this book for figurals may average a bit higher than those you have seen in other general and specific price guides, while prices of nonfigurals may run somewhat lower.

Keep in mind that the estimated values shown throughout the book are meant to be used simply as a guideline, and may vary from one part of the country to another. They may also slide up and down on specific pieces as collector interest in them rises or falls. Unless otherwise stated, prices are based on items being in mint condition with the exception of minor crazing. Note that all prices are in five dollar increments. **To arrive at prices I took what I thought each piece to be worth, then rounded it** *down* **to the last five dollars.** For example, if, after researching various price guides and listening to input from collectors and dealers, I determined a piece was worth $19, it will show an estimated value of $15. This was done because, without exception, all dealers I talked to who deal heavily in Royal Copley told me that for a year or so after the Wolfe's books were republished in 1992 Copley sold very well, but recently sales have been sluggish. For that reason rounding down may give a truer perspective of actual market value.

The best way to use the price guide is not to pinpoint a certain dollar amount, but to determine the relative value of one piece as opposed to another. As an example, the *Deer and Fawn Planter* shows a price of $45 with gold, $30 without it. Should interest in the piece rise, a collector may no longer be able to purchase it for those amounts. Should interest in the piece taper off, a dealer may no longer be able to sell it for those prices. Either way, it will probably always be worth significantly more money than the *Double Spray Planter* shown below it, which indicates a value of $10.

Copley prices in the future? Don't really know but it's certainly a subject worthy of a short discussion, the theme of which should be that collectibles are much better for collecting than they are for investing. As alluded to above, items usually become collectible several decades after they were made because of the nostalgic yearnings of those who grew up with them, and the increased appreciation of people in general. These two groups fuel interest in the collectible, whatever it may be, and watch prices rise for several years. Then one of two things happens. Either the collectible remains viable and eventually attains status as a genuine antique due to design quality, usefulness or ageless appeal, or it fades back into the very obscurity from which it arose. At the time of this writing, which way Copley will go is unknown because not enough time has elapsed.

Right now it's in the first stage of what we might call the life of a collectible, interest in it generated by those who remember it, and by those who have cast aside their former prejudice against it. In order for Copley to pass beyond that, these two groups are going to have to be joined by a third group, several years younger, which develops an appreciation based solely on aesthetics-style, design, decoration, etc., not previous exposure or current market trends. If that third group never coalesces, someday the prices of Copley may plummet.

So what it comes down to is that if you are collecting Royal Copley as a long term investment, you must consider it to be one of a highly speculative nature, far less stable than many other long term investments. You may not only fail to make any money, you may even lose some. You may gain, too, of course, but it remains to be seen. One thing is certain, you will not collect any dividends or interest during the years between the time you buy it and the time you sell it. On the other hand, if you collect Royal Copley solely because you appreciate its quality and design, enjoy the thrill of the hunt and take pride in owning and displaying beautiful objects, that makes you a collector in the truest sense of the word, and your rewards will be far greater and longer lasting than anything so trivial as monetary gain.

Throughout its life the Spaulding China Company did an apparently booming business in figural planters, assuming the large number that remains today is an accurate indicator. This *Cocker Spaniel with Basket Planter* is a typical example. Standing 5-1/2 inches high it carries a Shaffer gold stamp but no Spaulding identification. The piece has three runners. A similar planter without gold can be found on page 37. Estimated value: $25. *Osborne Collection.*

Take a stroll through any antique show or flea market today with Royal Copley on your mind and you will very soon realize that figural ware formed the heart of the Spaulding China Company's fiscal survival and profitability. Figural pieces outnumber nonfigural pieces by a large measure. That is not unusual. Aside from dinnerware and sanitary ware manufacturers, most mid-twentieth century potteries that lasted for any period of time at all staked their reputations and financial well-being on figurals.

Most Spaulding figurals can be divided into two broad categories, figurines and planters, which would include wallpockets. The company also pushed banks, and dabbled in figural ashtrays, lamps, and cream and sugar sets.

Spaulding China Company figural planters are generally of fairly large size, and quite heavy. The same holds true of many of its figurines.

Another big part of the company's business was figurines, such as this beautifully gold decorated *Royal Windsor Small Hen and Rooster.* The *Hen* is 6-3/4 inches high, the *Rooster* 7-1/4 inches. More hens and roosters appear on pages 45 through 52. Estimated value: $40 each. *Osborne Collection.*

The *Teddy Bear with Concertina Planter* stands 7-1/2 inches high. It is unmarked but has one runner on the bottom. Estimated value: $55. *Carson Collection.*

CHAPTER 4

ANIMALS

One thing about Spaulding's animals, you never have a problem recognizing the species. Bears are definitely bears, pigs are definitely pigs. The same cannot be said of its birds, a category in which even a naturalist might have a hard time differentiating a flycatcher from a swallow or a vireo.

Spaulding animals are true to life in shape, and run the gamut from natural to personified. Most of the time they were finished in colors that, if not exactly natural, were close enough to it that your brain will construe them as so. Once in a while the colors were bizarre, as with the pink poodle shown on page 31.

Teddy Bear with Mandolin Planter, 6-5/8 inches high, unmarked. Estimated value: $45. *Carson Collection.*

An unmarked *Teddy bear Figurine,* 5-5/8" high. Because of the slight change to a horizontally held sucker, the generally smooth texture of the fur, the fuzzy appearance of the eyes, etc., it is my opinion that this item, and its companion bank on page 10, may have been made exclusively by China Craft. Estimated value: not determined. *Osborne Collection.*

These *Teddy Bear with Sucker Planters,* are 8 inches high. Unmarked, it has a two runners. The darker color on the left is rarer than the lighter color on the right. Estimated value: left $45, right $35. *Carson Collection.*

These *Teddy Bear Planters* are similar to the previous example, but lack the sucker. They are smaller, too, 6-3/8 inches. Each has two runners, and is unmarked save for the Royal Copley paper label on the brown example. As above, white is rarer. Estimated value: left $25, right $65. *Carson Collection.*

The white *Teddy Bear Planter,* as shown on the left with a Royal Copley paper label, is very rare. The one on the right, with a pebble glaze, was made by China Craft after the Spaulding plant closed. As above, each piece is 8 inches high, and has two runners. Estimated value: left $85, right $35. *Carson Collection.*

Teddy Bear Banks, each 7-1/2 inches high, unmarked, and sporting two runners. Note that the one on the right is gold decorated. Estimated value: left $45, right $65. *Carson Collection.*

The unmarked *Teddy Bear on Tree Stump Planter* is 5-1/2 inches high. It has two runners. Estimated value: $20. *Carson Collection.*

As you might suspect from reading about the other white bears above, this is the rarest color of the *Teddy Bear in Basket Planter.* Estimated value: $75. *Osborne Collection.*

The *Bear Cub Clinging to Stump Planter* is 8-1/4 inches high. It has four runners, no mark. Sometimes the bear is seen in darker gray with the head being the same color instead of white. Estimated value: $30. *Carson Collection.*

Everything the same as at right, but with a pink scarf. Estimated value: $50. *Carson Collection*

Teddy Bear in Basket Planter, 8 inches high, unmarked, two runners. Estimated value: $50. *Carson Collection.*

This is the *Cat with Cello Planter,* or, as I have heard others refer to it, Pablo Catsals. It stands 8 inches high, has three runners and is unmarked. Estimated value: $60. *Carson Collection.*

The *Teddy Bear with Basket on Back Planters* stand 5-1/2 inches high. Neither is marked. The pink and blue one is harder to find than the brown and yellow one. Estimated value: left $45, right $30. *Carson Collection.*

The *Siamese Cats Planter* is extremely rare. The planter part is a basket behind the cats, a small part of which can be seen extending from the back of the feline on the right. Height is 9-1/2 inches; the planter is unmarked but has two runners. Although I have never seen it, it is possible this was also made in brown. Estimated value: $100. *Carson Collection.*

Another rare piece, the *Kitten and Birdhouse Planter* is 8-1/8 inches high, no mark, two runners. Estimated value: $65. *Carson Collection.*

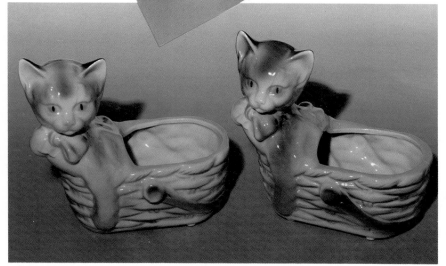

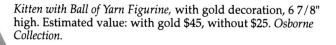
Kitten with Ball of Yarn Figurine, with gold decoration, 6 7/8"
high. Estimated value: with gold $45, without $25. *Osborne
Collection.*

Each of these *Kitten in Picnic Basket Planters* is unmarked, each
has two runners. There is a slight difference in height, 7-7/8
inches on the left, 8-1/8 inches on the right. That may be due
to several factors including substantially different firing
temperatures and different clay mixtures. The possibility also
exists that the original block, used to make the mold, was
recarved at some point and came out a little shorter or taller.
Estimated value: $45 each. *Carson Collection.*

The *Resting Cat Planter* is 5-3/4 inches
high. It has four runners, no mark.
Incidentally, if you ever see the word
recumbent used in regard to the position
of an animal figure, this is the position it
signifies. Estimated value: $35. *Carson
Collection.*

Kitten in Cradle Planter, 6-1/8 inches high. It is not marked and
has two runners. I suspect this may have been made with the
colors reversed, pink cradle blue blanket and ruffle, but have
not seen it that way. This planter, and the *Resting Cat Planter*
directly above, are good examples of rarity not necessarily
being the prime factor that determines Spaulding prices. Both
are rarer than the more expensive *Cat with Cello Planter,* but the
Cat with Cello Planter is more popular. Estimated value: $45.
Carson Collection.

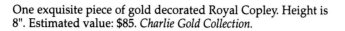

One exquisite piece of gold decorated Royal Copley. Height is 8". Estimated value: $85. *Charlie Gold Collection.*

Each of these brown *Cat Figurines* is 8 inches high. They are unmarked, and do not have runners. Estimated value: $35 each. *Carson Collection.*

The *Kitten with Ball of Yarn Figurine* on the left is 6 7/8" high. The *Kitten with Ball of Yarn Planter* on the right is 8" high. Neither is marked, both have three runners. Estimated value: left $35, right $25. *Carson Collection.*

Black *Cat Figurines* are more common than brown ones. Heights are 8 inches on the left, 8-1/4 inches on the right. Neither has runners. Estimated value: $25 each. *Carson Collection.*

The black *Cat Planter* is one of Spaulding's most commonly seen cats. It stands 8 inches high, sports three runners. Estimated value: $15. *Carson Collection.*

This is the *Kitten on Stump Planter*, 6-1/8 inches high. It has two runners, no other markings. Estimated value: $20. *Carson Collection.*

At first glance this looks like a light and dark version of the same *Kitten with Ball of Yarn Planter*, but that's not the case. Among the subtleties that make these two different planters is the angle of the horizontal yarn strands, orientation of the hole in the back, space between the ribbon and front paw, and the rear leg where it joins the tail. Study the picture carefully and you will find more. Height on the left is 8-1/8 inches, height on the right 8-3/8 inches. Neither is marked, each has three runners. Estimated value: $25 each. *Carson Collection.*

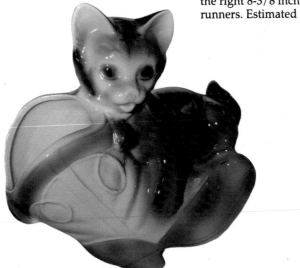

The *Kitten on Boot Planter* is 7-3/4 inches high, unmarked except for three runners. Estimated value: $20. *Carson Collection.*

Kitten with Moccasin Planter, 8-1/8 inches high with four runners. The only mark is the Royal Copley paper label on the moccasin. Estimated value: $30. *Carson Collection.*

There are three runners on the bottom of this *Kitten and Book Planter*. It stands 6-5/8 inches high. Estimated value: $20. *Carson Collection*.

The *White Deer on Sled Planter* is 6-3/4 inches high, has 3 runners and the number 292 impressed towards the bottom of the opposite side. This piece, although long considered to be Copley, may not be at all, as one has recently been found with a Stanfordware paper label. This would also casts doubt on the other pieces with impressed numbers, such as the *Lamb on Sled Planter*. On the other hand, both potteries were located in the same town and Stanfordware owner George Stanford at one time worked at Spaulding. It's altogether possible that one pottery did work for the other on a contract basis from time to time when a glut of orders necessitated it. Estimated value: not determined. *Carson Collection*.

This planter stands 7-3/8 inches high, has three runners but no mark. Like all of the baby ware items, it was also finished in blue. Estimated value: $20. *Carson Collection*.

If you ever found this 5-3/8 inches high *Black Cat and Tub Planter* in a different color scheme, you would have a very rare piece. Two runners, no mark. Estimated value: $15. *Carson Collection*.

Full-Bodied Deer on Stump Planter, 8-1/4 inches high. It has four runners but is not marked. Estimated value: $20. *Carson Collection*.

Note the Royal Copley paper label on this *Little Deer Head Vase*, 7-3/8 inches high. It has two runners. Estimated value: $20. *Carson Collection.*

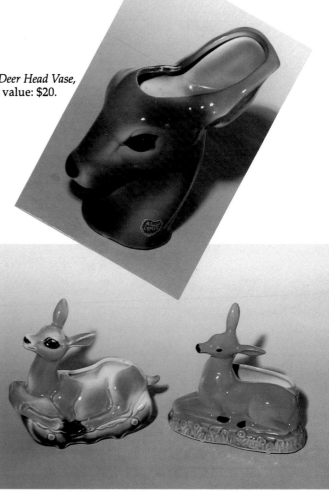

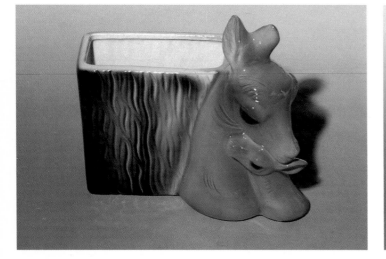

The *Deer and Fawn with Side Planter* is 7-1/2 inches high. It is not marked but does have three runners. It was also made in a smaller size. Estimated value: large $20, small $20. *Carson Collection.*

As explained on page 27, the origin of the *Deer on Sled Planter* has recently become questionable. It may not have been made by Spaulding. The 6-3/4" high unmarked *Resting Deer Planter* is probably not a Spaulding piece, either, although most collectors have long considered it to be. While it has two runners, one near the tail and one near the middle, under the front legs it has a disk-shaped dry foot which is inconsistent with the rest of the company's output. Also, the green has way too much yellow in it, and the brown doesn't seem to match, either. Estimated value: not determined. *Carson Collection.*

The *Deer and Fawn Planter,* on the left, is 9-1/2 inches high, has Royal Copley in raised letters on the bottom. The *Deer and Fawn Figurine,* on the right, stands 8-3/4 inches, also has Royal Copley in raised letters on the bottom. The planter with gold decoration appears on page 17. Estimated value: left $20, right $30. *Carson Collection.*

The *Dog with String Bass Planter* is one of Spaulding's most sought after dogs. It stands 7-1/4 inches high, has four runners on the bottom but no mark. Estimated value: $70. *Carson Collection.*

Both of these pieces, which average 8 inches in height, are foreign imports. The bank carries an inkstamp, "T1864," while the planter is stamped, T1863. The planter has been found with a Brinn's paper label. Brinn's is an import company based in Pittsburgh. Both pieces are much lighter in weight than similar sized Spaulding pieces. Estimated value: Not determined.

The pottery portion of this lamp is 11-3/8" high. The piece is not marked. All of the experts I have interviewed seem convinced it was made by Spaulding, but as yet must be considered unconfirmed as it has not been found with a paper label. Estimated value: not determined. *Courtesy of Fred Fatula.*

These 8-1/4 high *Dog at Mail Box Planters* are genuinely rare items in black and white, much, much harder to find than the standard variety shown below. The Planters have four runners, are not marked. Estimated value: without gold $75, with gold $90. *Carson Collection.*

The *Dog at Mailbox Planter,* in these standard colors, is rather common. It must have been popular with consumers. Height here averages 8-1/8 inches. The planters have four runners, no marks. Estimated value: $15. *Carson Collection.*

Pup in Picnic Basket Planter, 7-3/4 inches high, two runners, no mark. Estimated value: $45. *Carson Collection.*

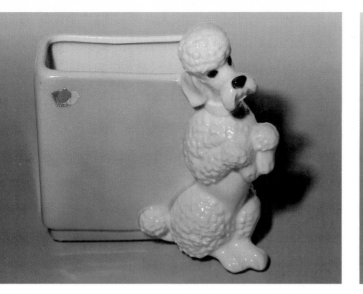

Erect White Poodle Planter, 6-3/8 inches high, unmarked but with a Royal Windsor paper label. Estimated value: $20. *Carson Collection.*

Erect White Poodle Planter in black. Estimated value: $20. *Carson Collection.*

The *Resting Poodle Planters* stand 6-1/2 inches high, have four runners. Note the Royal Copley paper label on the pink one. Estimated value: pink $55, gray $55. *Carson Collection.*

The *Resting Poodle Planter* in gray with gold decoration. Estimated value: $75. *Osborne Collection.*

Resting Poodle Planter in white, more common than the other colors. This was also made in blue, which is very rare. Estimated value: white $40, blue (not shown), $85. *Carson Collection.*

The poodle planters in green, which at Spaulding was pretty close to black. The one in the middle is called the *Sitting White Poodle Planter*. Estimated value: $20 each. *Carson Collection.*

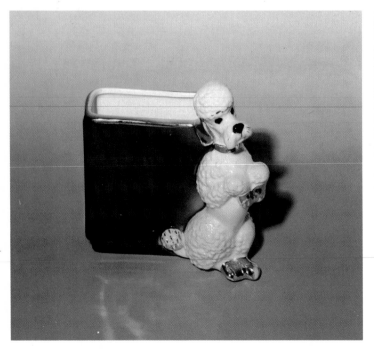

The *Erect White Poodle Planter* with gold is a nice find. Estimated value: $30. *Carson Collection.*

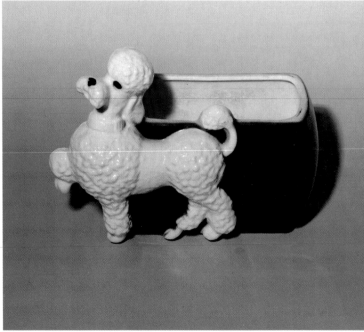

This is the *Prancing White Poodle Planter*. It is 6-1/4 inches high, has three runners. Estimated value: $20. *Carson Collection.*

The *Erect Poodle Planter* in baby ware is harder to find than the more generic versions shown above. It stands 6-3/8 inches high, has two runners, no mark. Note that the sides and back are finished in pink or blue glaze. Estimated value: $35 each. *Carson Collection.*

Posing Poodle with Bow Planter in another color scheme. Estimated value: $25. *Carson Collection.*

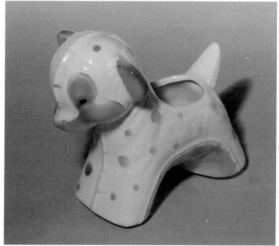

Same as above and, strictly speaking, also baby ware although I didn't do a very good job of photographing the one on the right, as you cannot see any of the pink that is on the sides and back. Estimated value: $25 each. *Carson Collection.*

This *Stuffed Animal Dog Planter* is 5 inches high, carries two runners, is not marked. Estimated value: $35. *Carson Collection.*

Called simply the *Dog Planter,* this item stands 7-3/4 inches high. It is un-marked, has three runners, and is easy to remember because it is the only dog planter or figurine that has one front foot off the ground. Estimated value: $30. *Carson Collection.*

The *Posing Poodle with Bow Planters* are 5-1/4 inches high. They have three runners, are unmarked. Estimated value: $25 each. *Carson Collection.*

This *Pup with Suitcase Planter* is 7 inches high. It has three runners, no mark, and the name Skip on the luggage tag. Estimated value: $20. *Carson Collection.*

Pup in Basket Planter. It stands 6-7/8 inches high, is not marked but has two runners. Estimated value: $20. *Carson Collection.*

The *Dog Figurines* on the left and right are 8-1/2 inches high. The *Dog Planter* in the middle is 8-5/8 inches high. While none of these pieces is marked, the planter does have three runners. Estimated value: Figurine $20, planter $15. *Carson Collection.*

Another piece called a *Dog Figurine.* This one is 6-7/8 inches high, has four runners, is unmarked. Estimated value: $20. *Carson Collection.*

These *Airedale Figurines* all stand 6-1/2 inches high. They are not marked. The color of the dog in the middle is more common than those of the dogs on the ends. Estimated value: middle $15, ends $20 each. *Carson Collection.*

Another *Dog Figurine,* possibly made as a mate for the one at the bottom of page 34. It is somewhat larger, 8-1/2 inches high, has three runners. Estimated value: $20. *Carson Collection.*

Spaniel Figurines, 6 inches high. Neither is marked save for the Royal Copley paper label on the lighter one, which is the more common color. Estimated value: dark $25, light $20. *Carson Collection.*

Another *Spaniel Figurine,* this one being 7-3/4 inches high. Estimated value: $20. *Carson Collection.*

Height of the *Dog Pulling Wagon Planter* is 5-7/8 inches high. It is not marked but does have three runners. Estimated value: $20. *Carson Collection.*

This is the *Cocker Spaniel Planter,* shown from both sides. Height is 8-1/4 inches. The one with the chocolate face is rare, the one with the tan face is common. Estimated value: chocolate face, $45, tan face $15. *Carson Collection.*

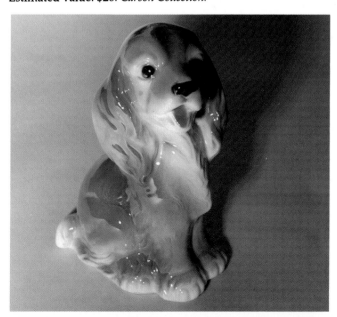

A 5-7/8 inch high *Spaniel Figurine*. It is not marked. Estimated value: $20. *Osborne Collection*.

What a wonderful example of how identical planters can be made to look so different. The words bold, aggressive and grumpy might be used to describe the dog on the left, while demure, affectionate or obedient would better suit the one on the right. The *Cocker Spaniel Planters* stand 7 inches high. They are unmarked. This same planter was also made in an 8-inch size. Estimated value: 7-inch $15, 8-inch (not shown) $15. *Carson Collection*.

Same as above but a darker shade of brown. Estimated value: $15 *Carson Collection*.

The *Cocker Spaniel Figurines* are 6-1/8 inches high, unmarked. This picture shows the same figurine from different angles. Note the slightly varying colors. Estimated value: $15 each. *Carson Collection*.

Cocker Head Planters, (wallpockets actually), 5 inches high. Each has Royal Copley in raised letters on the back. The color on the left is seen less often than the color on the right. Estimated value: left $20, right $15. *Carson Collection*.

The *Cocker Spaniel with Basket Planter* is quite common in the yellow, much rarer in the green. Height is 5 inches. Each has three runners, and the one on the left has a Shaffer gold stamp. Estimated value: left $25, center $30, right $15. *Carson Collection.*

The *Stuffed Animal Elephant Planter* stands 6-3/4 inches high, is unmarked but has two runners. Like all baby items it is somewhat rare. Estimated value: $40. *Carson Collection.*

Small Elephant with Ball Planter in gray. Estimated value: $20. *Carson Collection.*

These are the *Small* and *Large Elephant with Ball Planters*, 6-1/4 and 7-1/2 inches high. Each has two runners, neither is marked. Estimated value: small $20, large $25. *Carson Collection.*

This is the *Gazelle Planter*, 9 inches high, marked only by paper label. Estimated value: $25. *Carson Collection.*

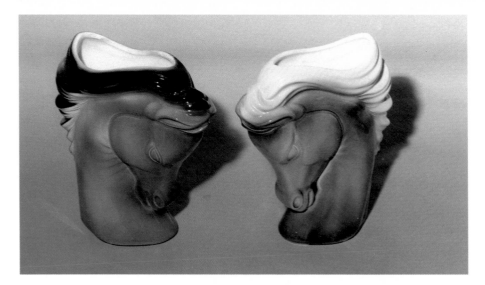

Called the *Horse with Mane Vase,* this piece stands 8-1/4 inches high, is unmarked, has three runners. The gray is seen more often than the brown. Estimated value: brown $25, gray $20. *Carson Collection.*

Named simply the *Horsehead Vase*, this piece is 6 inches high. It is not marked, has three runners. Estimated value: $15 each. *Carson Collection.*

The *Mare and Foal Vase*, shown from both sides. It is 8-1/2 inches high, has Royal Copley in raised lettering on the bottom. Estimated value: with gold $45, without gold $25. *Carson Collection.*

This horsehead ashtray measures 4-3/8 x 6-1/2 inches, has a Royal Windsor paper label and USA impressed on the bottom. Estimated value: $15. *Courtesy of Doris Dyer.*

Inkstamp of the Parky bank Note that it says 1958, while Spaulding closed up shop in 1957. This piece was possibly made by China Craft.

Three *Pig Banks,* each 7-3/4 inches high. None is marked with the exception of Parky, whose inkstamp is shown at right. Estimated value: $30 each. *Carson Collection.*

Large Pig Banks, 8-1/8 inches high. Neither is marked. Estimated value: $35 each. *Carson Collection.*

These are the same as those at left but apparently for the man of the house instead of the lady. Estimated value: $35 each. *Carson Collection.*

Different sizes here, 6-1/8 inches left and center, 5-1/2 inches on the right. None is marked. Estimated value: $25 each. *Carson Collection.*

Just for good measure let's toss in a pig lamp here. It is 6-1/8 inches high and unmarked. Estimated value: $45. *Osborne Collection.*

The banks on the outside are 7-5/8 inches high while the one on the inside stands 6-7/8 inches. All are unmarked. Estimated value: outside $30, inside $25. *Carson Collection.*

A *Pig Bank* made especially for someone named Samuel. It is 7-3/4 inches high, has a Royal Copley inkstamp. Estimated value: $35. *Osborne Collection.*

I took three shots of this trying to get something that wouldn't prove offensive but the camera lens failed to smooth out the wrinkles. What the verse really says is: Let me tuck / Your coins away / For what you'll want / To buy someday!

Three examples of the *Small Pig Bank,* each 4-3/4 high, unmarked. The paper label of the one on the right is shown below. Estimated value: $20 each. *Carson Collection.*

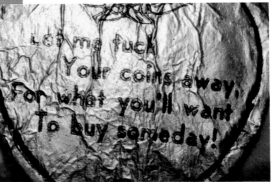

Those are *Farmer Pig Banks* on each end. They are 5-1/2 inches high, unmarked. They look enough like Shawnee's Smiley Pig cookie jar and shakers that you almost have to believe one was modeled after another. Who copied whom? I would have to put my money on Spaulding having been the copycat for two reasons. According to Jim and Bev Mangus in *Shawnee Pottery — An Identification and Value Guide* (Collector Books, 1994), Shawnee designers Rudy Ganz and Ed Hazel modeled their original Smiley in 1942, the year Spaulding was just getting underway, from an image Ganz saw in a child's picture book. Also, according to the Wolfes (Book II page 14), vice president Irving Miller made a habit of basing new Spaulding designs on pieces already being produced by other potteries. The three pieces on the inside are called *Bow Tie Pig Banks*. They stand 6-1/4 inches high, are not marked. Estimated value: *Farmer Pig Banks* $40 each, *Bow Tie Pig Banks* $25 each. *Carson Collection.*

No doubt about when this *Pig Bank* was made. It stands 4-3/4 inches high, is not marked. Estimated value: $25. *Osborne Collection.*

Bow Tie Pig Bank with closed eyes. Like the three above, it is unmarked. Height is 6-1/2 inches. Estimated value: $35. *Osborne Collection.*

Pig Creamers, 4-3/8 inches high, "Pat. Pending," impressed in the bottom. According to the Wolfes, some are found with "Spaulding Pat. 113726," impressed. Interesting. Design patent no. 113726 corresponds to a date of 1939, which is a couple years before the generally agreed to starting date for the Spaulding China Company. Perhaps the company purchased the design from a freelancer who had previously patented it. Both of these creamers are identical; the tams look different because they were photographed from opposite sides. Estimated value: $15 each. *Carson Collection.*

One of three different *Buntings* Spaulding made, this example stands 4-3/4 inches high. It is not marked. Estimated value: $20. *Carson Collection.*

Here's number two among the *Buntings,* 5-1/8 high, also unmarked. Original price tag on this read 49-cents. *Bunting* no. 3 is a wallpocket that can be found in Chapter 8. Estimated value: $20. *Carson Collection.*

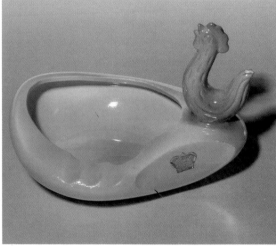

Rooster Banks. Heights left to right are 8-1/4, 8-1/8 and 8-1/4 inches. Although hard to see, they say Chicken Feed across the front of their bases. The one in the center has not been verified as Spaulding. It is marked, Chicken Feed, Reg. U.S. Pat. Office, Vic Moran, Bradford PA. Estimated value: outside $40 each, inside not determined. *Carson Collection.*

Rooster ashtray similar to the horsehead ashtray on page 39. Height to the top of the ashtray is 2 inches, to the top of the rooster 4-5/8 inches. This piece is not marked except for the Royal Windsor paper label. Estimated value: $15. *Carson Collection.*

The *Chick Creamers* are 5 inches high, have Pat-Pending impressed and Spaulding paper labels. Estimated value: $15 each. *Carson Collection.*

This is the *Small Royal Copley Hen and Rooster* no. 1, 5-5/8 and 6 inches high, respectively. They are unmarked. Estimated value: $15 each. *Carson Collection.*

The *Small Royal Copley Hen and Rooster no. 1* in white and black. Heights of these, 5-1/2 and 5-3/4 inches, are just a bit different than those above which is a common occurrence. Estimated value: $40 each. *Carson Collection.*

Whenever you see a designation such as *Small Royal Copley Hen and Rooster no. 1*, you can bet that a *Small Royal Copley Hen and Rooster no. 2* is lurking close behind, and here they are. Each is 6-1/4 inches high, neither is marked. Estimated value: $15 each. *Carson Collection.*

6-1/4" high *Royal Windsor Hen* with gold trim. Estimated value: $30. *Carson Collection.*

Small *Royal Copley Hen and Rooster no.* 2 with gold trim. Estimated value: $35 each. *Carson Collection.*

Known as the *Small Royal Windsor Hen and Rooster,* this pair is 6-5/8 and 7-1/4 inches. They are not marked. Estimated value: $15 each. *Carson Collection.*

Royal Windsor Chickens, 7-1/4 and 6-3/4 inches high, respectively. They are not marked. Estimated value: $15 each. *Carson Collection.*

That is the *Small Royal Windsor Hen* on the left with a slightly different color treatment. The rooster matches the one shown immediately below. Estimated value: hen, $15, rooster, not determined. *Carson Collection.*

This is the same rooster that is shown directly above, plus a hen to match. The hen is 6-1/4 inches high, the rooster is 6-3/4 inches. Both are marked with an impressed U.S.A. on the rim of the base. Because of the mark and its location, along with the intricate mold detail on the tails, I am not yet ready to state positively that these are Copley. Estimated value: not determined. *Carson Collection.*

This rooster figurine is 7-3/4 inches high, unmarked. Note the pierced tail and vee at the back of the comb for field identification of this rare piece. Although I have never seen it, somewhere there must be a hen to go with it. Estimated value: $40. *Osborne Collection.*

This 7 inch rooster is unmarked except for the Royal Copley paper label visible on the front of the base. Estimated value: $25. *Carson Collection.*

The *Large Royal Copley Rooster and Hen* stand 8-1/4 and 7-1/2 inches high. Each is unmarked but has two runners. Estimated value: $20 each. *Carson Collection.*

Deeper colors, and a green tip on the tail of the rooster instead of brown. Estimated value: $20 each. *Carson Collection.*

A white and black version of the Large Royal Copley Hen and Rooster. Note the green bases. Estimated value: $45 each. *Carson Collection.*

And now white bases, a characteristic most collectors I interviewed considered a bona fide difference worthy of searching for. Estimated value: $50 each. *Carson Collection.*

Medium Size Royal Windsor Hen, 8 inches high and unmarked. Estimated value: $40. *Carson Collection.*

Large Royal Windsor Rooster, browner brown, grayer green, paler yellow than on the pair immediately below. Estimated value: $80. *Carson Collection.*

This is the *Large Royal Windsor Hen and Rooster.* Heights are 9-3/4 and 10-3/4 inches. They are unmarked. Estimated value: $80 each. *Carson Collection.*

Very similar to the *Large Royal Windsor Rooster* at first glance but far different. Not only is it shorter, 8-1/4 inches compared to 10-3/4 inches, but check the differences in the combs, wattles and tails. Estimated value: $40. *Osborne Collection.*

I used to think the *Royal Windsor 10-3/4-inch Rooster* shown above (and here for size comparison) was the tallest rooster Spaulding made. But that was before I saw this 11-1/2 inch version on the left. It's mammoth. It is also unmarked. And what does the hen that goes with it look like? Estimated value: left $120, right $80. *Osborne Collection.*

The *Rooster Vase* is 7-1/4 inches high. It is not marked but does have two runners. Estimated value: $15. *Carson Collection.*

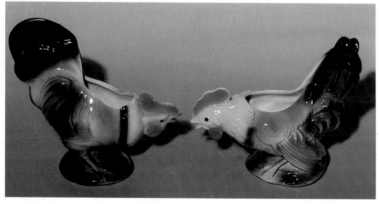

The piece on the left is the *Common Rooster Planter,* 7-1/8 inches high. The one on the right is the *Fighting Cock Planter,* one inch shorter. Each is unmarked, each has two runners. Estimated value: *Common* $15, *Fighting* $20. *Carson Collection.*

Two more *Common Rooster Planters,* the one on the left exhibiting a touch of handpainting. Too bad the glazing on its comb and wattle was so poorly executed. Estimated value: $15 each. *Carson Collection.*

Common Rooster Planter in white and black. This one has Royal Copley in raised letters on the bottom. Estimated value: $30. *Carson Collection.*

This *Rooster Planter* stands 8-3/8 inches high, while the *Hen Planter* is 8-1/4 inches. They are not marked. Estimated value: $15 each. *Carson Collection.*

The *Rooster Vase* is 7-1/4 inches high. It is not marked but does have two runners. Estimated value: $15. *Carson Collection.*

ARE THEY OR AREN'T THEY?

This unmarked pair of shakers, 4-1/2 and 5-1/8 inches high, has not been verified and may indeed not have been made by Spaulding. Rather than leave them out, they have been included to see if a reader can come up with a pair having a paper label to positively identify them as Copley, or perhaps another company. Estimated value: not determined. *Carson Collection.*

As you have already seen, Spaulding did not turn out an abundance of stylized animal designs, preferring most of the time to make its creatures natural, once in a while personified. Here, however, is a stylized rooster planter whose glaze and runners leave no doubt about its origin. It is 7-1/2 inches high, marked with a raised USA, and has two runners. Estimated value: $15. *Osborne Collection.*

While the *Cockatiel Planter* on the right appears at first to be the same as above, note that it has a green base instead of a black one. Estimated value: $20 each. *Carson Collection.*

The *Cockatiel Planter* stands 8-1/2 inches high. It is not marked, has three runners. Estimated value: $20. *Carson Collection.*

Again, looks the same but isn't as the height is only 6-1/2 inches. Note, too, the relative positions of the tails to the bases. The planter on the right is unmarked, the one on the left has a Shaffer gold stamp. Estimated value: left $25, right $15. *Carson Collection.*

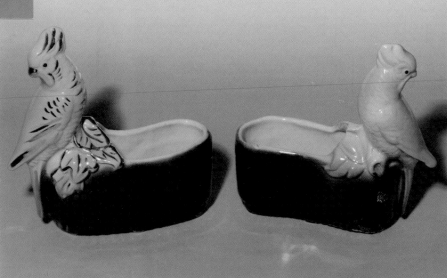

Not surprisingly, this is the *Large Cockatoo,* 8-1/4 inches high. Both have Royal Copley in raised letters on the bottom, and the one on the right has a Royal Copley paper label. Estimated value: $30 each. *Carson Collection.*

The *Double Birds on Tree Stump Figurine* stands 6-1/4 inches high. These pieces are marked by paper label only. Estimated value: $30. *Carson Collection.*

Three different treatments of the *Small Cockatoo.* Each is 7-3/4 inches high. All three are unmarked. Estimated value: $15 each. *Carson Collection.*

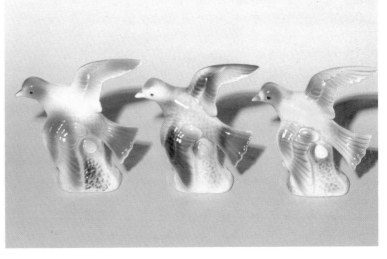

Two more renditions of the *Double Birds on Tree Stump Figurines.* Estimated value: $30 each. *Carson Collection.*

Rolling on through Spaulding's fantasy aviary, this picture shows three *Dove Figurines,* each 4-7/8 inches high. None is marked. Estimated value: $15 each. *Carson Collection.*

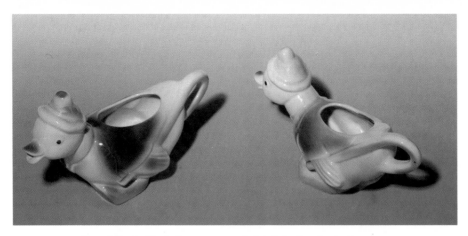

Spaulding's *Duck Creamers* stand 4-1/2 inches high. Some are marked, some are not. In this picture the one on the left has Pat. Pending, impressed in the bottom while the one on the right has Spaulding / Pat. 113725. Estimated value: $15 each. *Carson Collection.*

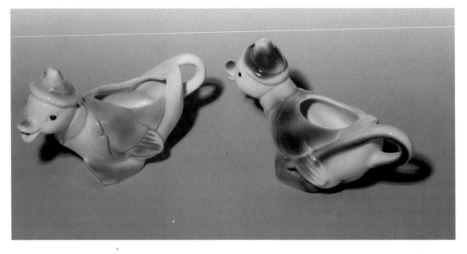

Two more *Duck Creamers.* Marks were not recorded. Estimated value: $15 each. *Carson Collection.*

This is the *Gadwell Drake and Hen* from the *A.D. Priolo Game Birds of America Series,* which is widely felt to be some of Spaulding's finest work. The hen is 7 inches high, the drake 8-3/4 inches. Both are marked, U.S.A. being impressed in each bottom, and A.D. Priolo impressed in the rim of the bottom. Anthony D. Priolo was a designer who did work for Spaulding. Estimated value: $60 each. *Carson Collection.*

The *Green-Winged Teal* are the rarest of the three large and one small set that comprise the *Game Birds of America Series*. The hen is 8 inches high, the drake 8-3/4 inches. They are marked the same as the *Gadwells*. Estimated value: $70 each. *Carson Collection*.

Mallard Ducklings, Drake and Hen, to go with the *A.D. Priolo Mallards* shown below. Heights are 5-3/4 and 4-1/8 inches. Each has "U.S.A." impressed on the rim of the bottom. Note that the tips of the wings have been chipped on this particular pair. As far as is known, the *Mallards* are the only species in the series for which ducklings were made. Estimated value: $30 each (if perfect). *Carson Collection*.

The *Mallards*, the most commonly found of the *Game Birds of America Series*. The drake stands 8-1/2 inches, the hen 6-3/4 inches. Marked as the other large Priolo ducks. Estimated value: $50 each. *Carson Collection*.

On the left is the *Mallard Drake* in a slightly different color treatment, on the right the *Green-Winged Teal Drake* with a white head. Estimated value: *Mallard* $50, *Green-Winged Teal* $70. *Carson Collection.*

Mallard Drake Figurine, 7-1/4 inches high, with two runners. It is unmarked. Estimated value: $20. *Carson Collection.*

Probably Spaulding's most common ducks, the *Erect Head Mallard* on the left and the *Bending Head Mallard* on the right. Heights are 9-1/4 and 9 inches, respectively. They are not marked. China Craft made this same set, along with the ducklings that go with it, at least as late as 1972, possibly later. They are shown in a Top Value Stamps Premium Catalog from that year, where they are attributed to China Craft. The coloring of the China Craft pieces is generally much less vivid than what you see here, especially the green on the head, which is often not much darker than the pale area immediately above the collar of this *Erect Head.* Check the China Craft *Sitting Mallard Planter* on page 58 and you will see exactly what I am talking about. Estimated value: Spaulding $25 each, China Craft (not shown) $10 each. *Carson Collection.*

Here is the *Baby Erect Head Mallard* and the *Baby Bending Head Mallard,* 5-3/4 and 5-1/4 inches high. They are unmarked except for the Royal Windsor paper label on the *Erect Head.* Like their larger counterparts above, the value depends upon them being Spaulding, not China Craft. Estimated value: Spaulding $10 each, China Craft $5 each. *Carson Collection.*

Mallard Duck on Stump Planter, 8-1/2 inches high, four runners, no mark. My experience has been that while this planter is fairly easy to find, it is fairly hard to find it in excellent condition. Estimated value: $20. *Carson Collection.*

Above right: By now you have no doubt come to admire the collection of Linley and Joyce Carson, which accounts for most of the pictures in the book. Of all the pieces shown, Linley Carson states that this *Duck and Mailbox Planter,* 6-7/8 inches high with two runners, is probably his favorite. Estimated value: $45. *Carson Collection.*

Right: Much smaller than the *Duck and Mailbox Planter* above, the *Duck and Wheelbarrow Planter* is only 3-3/4 inches high. It has two runners. Its only mark is a Royal Copley paper label. Estimated value: $15. *Carson Collection.*

A little different name here: *Mature Wood Duck Planter*. Height is 7-1/2 inches. The piece has three runners, no mark. Estimated value: $20. *Carson Collection*.

Two renditions of the *Mallard Duck Planter*, one plain, the other with gold trim which makes it a much more valuable piece on today's market. These planters are 8-1/2 inches high. Each is unmarked, each has three runners. Estimated value: plain $10, gold $30. *Carson Collection*.

Same as above, different colors. Estimated value: $20. *Carson Collection*.

The *Duck Eating Grass Planter* is one that eludes me—I've seen it only twice—but must not be that rare as most collectors place a rather low value on it. Height is 5-1/4 inches. It is unmarked, has two runners. Estimated value: $15. *Carson Collection*.

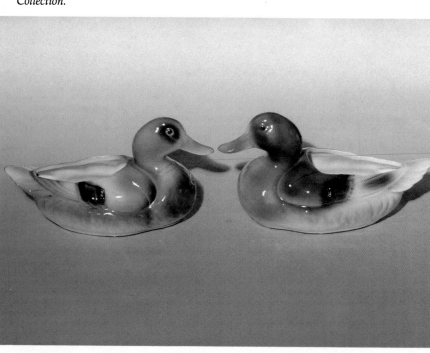

The *Sitting Mallard Planter* on the left has a China Craft paper label. Note that it is not done nearly as nicely as the identical Spaulding piece on the right. Although it doesn't show in the picture, the glaze is even chipping off of the China Craft piece. But the real giveaway, even if this planter did not have a China Craft paper label, is the green on the head. It's the same pale green that China Craft used for its version of the *Erect Head* and *Bending Head Mallards*. The planter on the left is 5 x 9-1/2 inches. The one on the right, 5-1/4 x 9-7/8 inches. Both have three runners. Estimated value: China Craft $5, Spaulding $20. *Carson Collection*.

This is the unmarked *Wood Duck Planter,* 5-3/4 inches high. It has two runners. Estimated value: $15 each. *Carson Collection.*

The *Stuffed Animal Duck Planter,* 6-1/4 inches high. It is not marked, has two runners. Estimated value: $30. *Carson Collection.*

Smoking Set. The *Large Ashtray* measures 3-1/4 x 6 inches. The two *Small Ashtrays* are 2-1/2 x 4-1/4 inches. All three pieces have no marks, two runners, and Royal Windsor paper labels. Estimated value: small $10 each, large $15. *Carson Collection.*

Here is the *Large Ashtray* with the pebble glaze used by China Craft. Estimated value: $10. *Osborne Collection.*

This *Large Ashtray* is 3-1/8 x 5-3/4 inches; slightly smaller than that shown above. My feeling is that it's probably China Craft as the quality does not measure up to Spaulding's usual high standard. Estimated value: $5.

The *Big Apple and Finch Planter,* 6-1/2 inches high, three runners, no mark. Estimated value: $15. *Carson Collection.*

Another finch, the *Finch on Tree Stump Planter.* It is 7-3/4 inches high, unmarked. It has three runners. Estimated value: $35. *Carson Collection.*

We round out the finch category with three *Finch Figurines,* all unmarked, all 5-1/8 inches high. Estimated value: $20 each. *Carson Collection.*

This is a *Flycatcher Figurine,* 8 inches high, unmarked. Estimated value: $20. *Carson Collection.*

These *Flycatchers* are also unmarked. Note the handpainted toenails, legs and head of the one on the left. Estimated value: left $25, right $20. *Carson Collection.*

While the *Goldfinch on Stump Planter* is by no means rare, the one on the right, with heavy gold decoration, is a premium example. Height is 6-3/4 inches. Both of these planters are unmarked. Both have three runners. Estimated value: plain $15, gold decorated $30. *Carson Collection.*

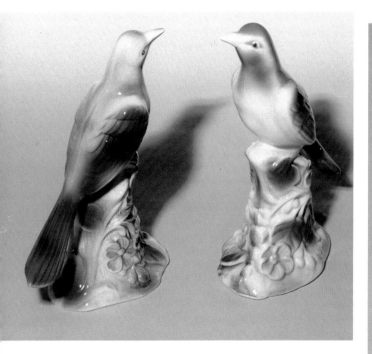

A couple more color combinations for the *Flycatchers,* a couple different angles from which to view them. Estimated value: $20 each. *Carson Collection.*

Here is the *Flycatcher* with a little fancier finish, similar to the one above with the handpainting. Estimated value: $25. *Osborne Collection.*

A pair of identical *Gull Figurines,* one from the front, the other from the back. They are 8 inches high, unmarked save for a Spaulding paper label not seen in the photo. Estimated value: $25 each. *Carson Collection.*

Not a bluejay, green jay or magpie jay but simply a *Jay,* this figurine is 8-1/2 inches high. It is not marked except by a Royal Copley paper label, the corner of which is barely visible below the bird's left foot. Estimated value: $20. *Carson Collection.*

Three more *Gull Figurines,* same size as above. Note the special treatment of the eyes on the two outside ones. Estimated value left and right $30, middle $25. *Osborne Collection.*

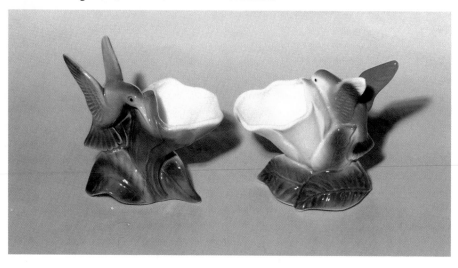

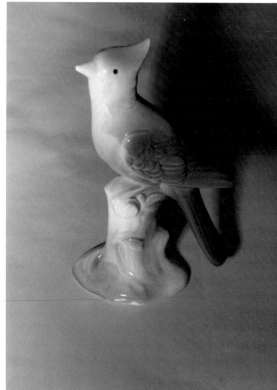

The *Hummingbird on Flower Planters* are 5-3/8 inches high, unmarked. Estimated value: $30 each. *Carson Collection.*

The *Jay* in a different color combination. Estimated value: $20. *Osborne Collection.*

Spaulding made two types of *Kingfisher Figurines,* this type being 5-1/8 inches high and unmarked. Estimated value: $20 each. *Carson Collection.*

A *Jay* with handpainted highlights is an unusual find. Estimated value: $40. *Osborne Collection.*

Kingfisher Figurine type 2, also unmarked, and 5 inches high. Estimated value: $20 each. *Carson Collection.*

Kinglet Planters, 5-1/8 inches high. The left one is not marked. The right one has a Shaffer gold stamp. Estimated value: plain $10, gold $25.

A matched pair of *Kingfishers.* Estimated value: single $20, matched pair $50. *Osborne Collection.*

The *Kinglet* is only 3-1/2 inches high. It is unmarked. Estimated value: $20. *Carson Collection.*

Two *Large Larks,* each 6 1/2" high, with the one on the left bearing a Spaulding paper label. Estimated value: $10 each. *Carson Collection.*

Small Lark Figurine in blue and tan. Estimated value: $5. *Osborne Collection.*

Collectors who choose to may acquire a never ending variety of the same piece, such as this *Kinglet* which is almost identical to the one above except for the white base. Estimated value: $20. *Osborne Collection.*

The Large Lark Figurine in another color scheme. Estimated value: $10. *Carson Collection.*

Small Lark Figurine with a Royal Copley paper label. Estimated value: $5. *Carson Collection.*

The *Small Lark Figurine,* is only 5 inches high, and unmarked. In the part of the country where I frequent antique shows and flea markets (Ohio, eastern Indiana, southern Michigan, western Pennsylvania) this is probably the most common Spaulding bird figurine. Estimated value: $5. *Carson Collection.*

Several *Large Larks,* this time one of them having a Royal Copley paper label. Estimated value: $10 each. *Carson Collection.*

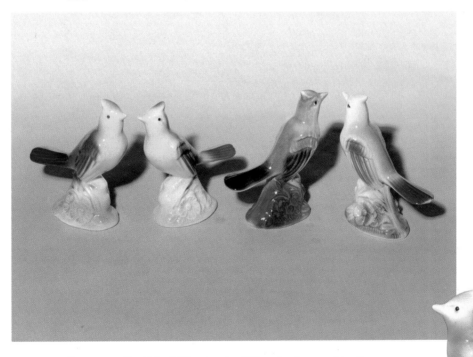

Four more *Small Lark Figurines* in different color combinations. Estimated value: $5 each. *Carson Collection.*

Last but not least, the *Baby Lark Figurine.* It is 3-5/8 inches high, unmarked. It is not only the smallest of Spaulding's larks, it is also the hardest to find. Estimated value: $20. *Carson Collection.*

The *Nuthatch* is another very common bird figurine. It is unmarked, and 5 inches high. Estimated value: $10 each. *Carson Collection.*

The *Double Parakeets* mounted on a lamp base. Estimated value: $45. *Carson Collection.*

A pair of *Double Parakeet Figurines* in different color treatments. Something else is different, too—one of them has a Spaulding inkstamp on the bottom. Estimated value: $35 each. *Carson Collection.*

This *Double Parakeet Figurine* stands 7-1/2 inches high. It is not marked. It is also not exceptionally common. Estimated value: $35. *Carson Collection.*

The *Nuthatch Planter* from both sides. Height is 5-1/2 inches. Unmarked but three runners. Estimated value: $10 each. *Carson Collection.*

Parrot Bud Vases, each 5" high. Two are unmarked, the third has a Royal Copley inkstamp. Estimated value: $10 each. *Carson Collection.*

This *Parrot Bud Vase* has Royal Copley impressed in the bottom. Estimated value: $10. *Carson Collection.*

Two more *Parrot Figurines.* Estimated value: $30 each. *Carson Collection*

This is a *Parrot Figurine,* 8 inches high, unmarked, Royal Copley paper label. Estimated value: $30. *Carson Collection.*

Spaulding's *Large Pheasant Hen Figurine* (left) measures 6-3/4 x 12 inches, the *Large Pheasant Cock Figurine* (right) 10-1/2 x 9 inches. They are not marked. Estimated value: $20 each. *Carson Collection.*

67

The *Large Pheasants,* apparently the ringneck variety, the kind most often seen in America. Size is the same as above. Note the stronger yellow on the male and the additional color on the bases. Estimated value: $20 each. *Carson Collection.*

Same birds as above but undecorated. Estimated value: $10 each. *Carson Collection.*

The *Pouter Pigeon Planter* stands 6-1/8 inches high, is unmarked, has two runners. Estimated value: $20 each. *Carson Collection.*

These smaller *Pheasant Figurines* measure 5-1/4 inches high. They are not marked. Estimated value: $15 each. *Carson Collection.*

A sparrow lamp. Note the Royal Copley paper label. Estimated value: $20. *Carson Collection*

68

Still smaller *Pheasant Figurines,* this time only 4-1/8 inches
high. Like those above, it is unmarked. Estimated value: $15
each. *Carson Collection.*

A small flock of *Sparrows.* Estimated value: $5 each. *Carson
Collection.*

Sparrow Figurines stand 5" high. They are unmarked except by
paper label. As you can see above *Sparrows* were made in many
color combinations. Estimated value: $5. *Carson Colection.*

Spaulding made five birds that have been labeled *Swallows*. These are the *Swallows on Heavy Double Stump Figurines*, 7-3/8" high and unmarked. Note that this picture shows two different figurines, a left version and a right version. Estimated value: $20 each. *Carson Collection.*

Swallow on Heavy Double Stump Figurine with gold decoration. Not surprisingly, it carries a Shaffer gold stamp. Estimated value: $35. *Carson Collection.*

Three *Swallows* from different angles. Estimated value: $15 each. *Carson Collection.*

This *Swallow Figurine* is almost the same size as those above, standing 7-1/2 inches high but that is where the similarity ends. It is not marked. Estimated value: $15. *Carson Collection.*

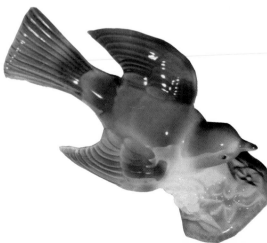

Blue *Swallow,* brown back. Estimated value: $15. *Osborne Collection.*

Two more *Swallows*. Estimated value: $15 each. *Carson Collection.*

A *Swallow* lamp, a nice addition to any collection. Estimated value: $30. *Carson Collection.*

These are *Hunt's Swallow Variant Male Figurines,* each 7-7/8 inches high. The female is shown below. In case you are wondering why you cannot find *Hunt's Swallow Variant* in any bird book, it is because the Wolfes named the figurines in honor of a friend or acquaintance. Estimated value: $30 each. *Carson Collection.*

Hunt's Swallow Variant Female, 8 inches high, with a Royal Copley paper label. Estimated value: $30. *Osborne Collection.*

Two more *Hunt's Swallow Variant Females,* same as above except one of them has a Spaulding paper label. Estimated value: $30 each. *Osborne Collection.*

This is the *Swallow with Extended Wings*. It is 7-1/4 inches high, unmarked. Two more *Swallows with Extended Wings* may be seen on page 9. Estimated value: $45. *Carson Collection.*

The *Tanager Planter*, which is seen quite often, measures 6 inches in height. It is marked Royal Copley in raised letters on the bottom. Estimated value: $10. *Carson Collection.*

The *Thrush Figurine* is a very common bird. It stands 6-3/8 inches high, is unmarked. Estimated value: $5. *Carson Collection.*

Three *Tanager Planters,* same size and mark as the picture at top right. Estimated value: $10 each. *Carson Collection.*

Three more *Thrushes*. Estimated value: $5 each. *Carson Collection*.

This is the *Titmouse Figurine*, 8-1/4 inches high and Estimated value: $15. *Carson Collection*.

Spaulding never seemed to run out of color combinations for its birds. Although *Thrushes* are common, you might find yourself having to pay a slight premium for brightly colored ones such as the yellow and blue example in this picture. That is not only true of the *Thrushes*, but of all Spaulding birds, or all Spaulding pieces for that matter. Estimated value: $5 each. *Carson Collection*.

Some more colorful renditions of the *Titmouse*. Estimated value: $20 each. *Carson Collection*.

Here's a beautiful pair of *Titmice* complete with handpainted highlights, something you do not see every day on Spaulding China Company figurines. Estimated value: $30 each. *Carson Collection.*

This *Vireo Figurine* is 4-3/8 inches high, unmarked, and very common. Estimated value: $5. *Carson Collection.*

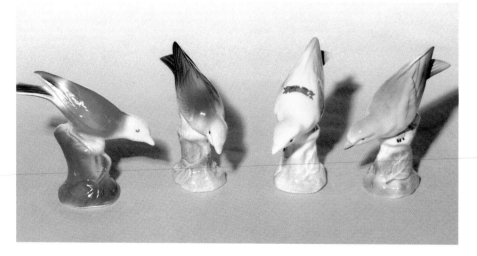

The decal across the back of the yellow *Vireo* in this picture indicates it was a souvenir of a tourist area. Estimated value: $5 each. *Carson Collection.*

Three more *Vireos* in different colors. Estimated value: $5 each. *Carson Collection.*

The *Warbler Bud Vase* stands 5 inches high. This example is marked Royal Copley in raised letters on the bottom. Estimated value: $10. *Carson Collection.*

All three of these *Warbler Bud Vases* are marked, the two on the outside with Royal Copley in raised letters on the bottom, the one in the center with a Royal Copley inkstamp. Estimated value: $10 each. *Carson Collection.*

This is the *Woodpecker Planter,* 6-1/4 inches high. It not only carries a Royal Copley paper label, it also has Royal Copley in raised letters on the bottom. Estimated value: $15. *Carson Collection.*

Two more *Woodpecker Planters,* shown from different angles.
Estimated value: $15 each. *Carson Collection.*

These *Little Wrens* are only 3-3/8 inches high. They are not marked, and were made with two different bottoms which are shown below. Estimated value: $15 each. *Carson Collection.*

Examples of the closed and open bottoms of the *Little Wrens.*

The *Little Wrens* in two other color schemes. Estimated value: $15 each. *Osborne Collection.*

The *Wren Figurine,* as opposed to the *Little Wren Figurines.* Height is 6-1/4 inches. *Wren Figurines* are unmarked except by paper label. Estimated value: $15. *Carson Collection.*

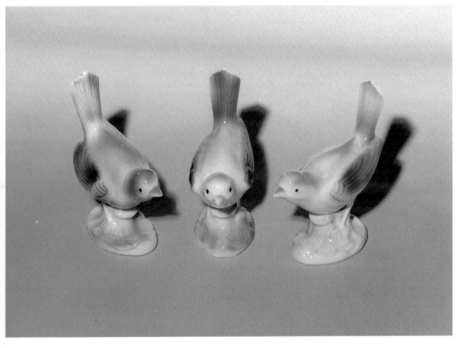

Three *Wren Figurines* with different color treatments. Estimated value: $15 each. *Carson Collection.*

A *Wren Figurine* lamp to illuminate your Spaulding treasures. Estimated value: $30. *Carson Collection.*

Three more colors. Estimated value: $15 each. *Carson Collection.*

More *Wrens,* more colors. Estimated value: $15
Collection.

This is the *Wren on Tree Stump Planter.* It is 6-1/2 inches high, has three runners but is not marked. Estimated value: $15. *Carson Collection.*

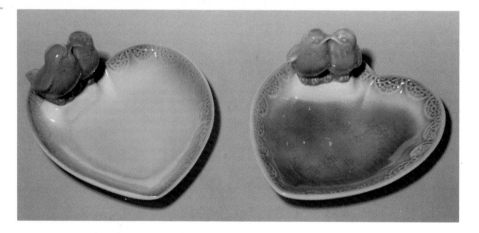

The *Affectionate Birds Ashtrays* are 5-1/2 inches across, have Royal Copley in raised letters on their bottoms. Estimated value: $5 each. *Carson Collection.*

These are *Leaf and Bird Ashtrays,* 5-3/8 inches in diameter. They have Royal Copley inkstamp marks. Estimated value: $5 each. *Carson Collection.*

The *Lily Pad with Bird Ashtray* on the left is 2-1/8 inches high including the bird, 1-1/4 inches not including it. Mark is a Royal Copley inkstamp. The *Small Bowl with Perched Bird* is 2-1/2 inches high to the top of the rim, 4-1/8 inches high to the top of the bird. It carries a Royal Copley inkstamp. Estimated value: $5 each. *Carson Collection.*

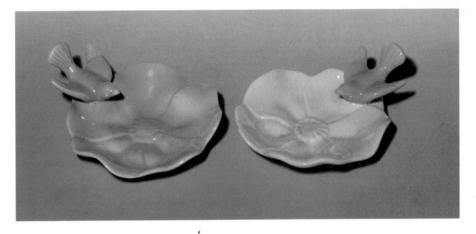

Lily Pad with Bird Ashtray in a couple other colors. Estimated value: $5 each. *Carson Collection.*

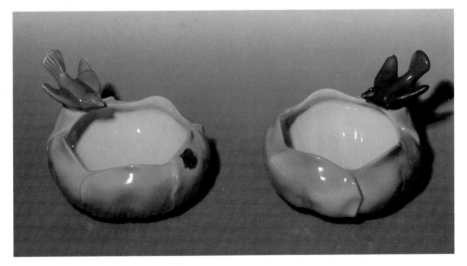

Two more examples of the *Small Bowl with Perched Bird.* The one on the right is marked with a Royal Copley inkstamp. Only mark of the one on the left is the Royal Copley paper label. Estimated value: $5 each. *Carson Collection.*

The anniversary book is 4-3/4 inches high, is marked by "USA" in raised letters. Height of the birthday book is 4-1/2 inches. It has the standard mark. Estimated value: $5 each. *Carson Collection.*

Both of these books display The Lord's Prayer. They are 4-5/8 inches high, have standard marks. Estimated value: $5 each. *Carson Collection.*

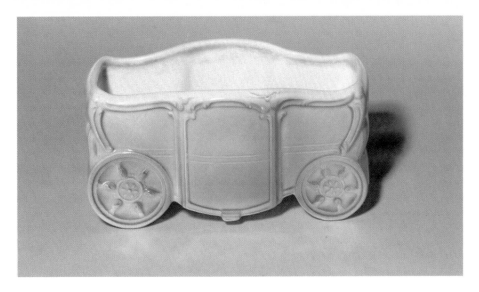

The *Coach Planter* stands 3-1/4 inches high, has only one runner, and carries a Royal Copley inkstamp. It appears the same on each side. Estimated value: $10. *Osborne Collection.*

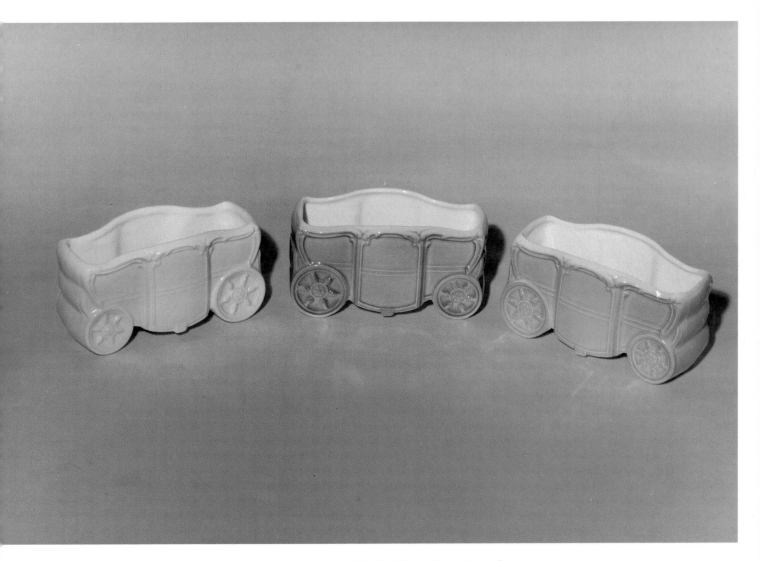

Three more *Coach Planters* with all of their vital statistics being the same as above. Estimated value: $10 each. *Carson Collection.*

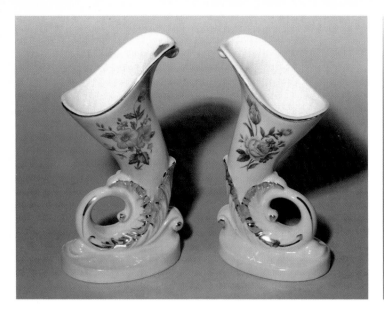

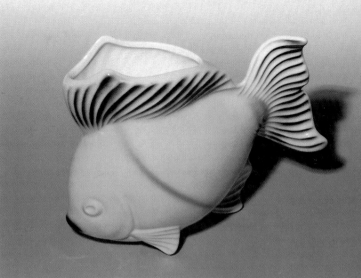

I tried arranging this pair with the pair above to show the difference in size but fitting them all in the same picture made them so small that a loss of detail resulted. Anyway, the heights are very different from those above, 6-1/2 inches on the left, 6-3/8 inches on the right. Collectors refer to this color as butterscotch. This pair illustrates perfectly why we cannot put too much stock in the designations Royal Copley, Royal Windsor and Spaulding. Generally considered to be a Spaulding product, the vase on the left has a Spaulding paper label along with a Reg. Pat'd gold stamp. The vase on the right carries the logo Royal Copley in raised letters on its bottom. While an employee may have inadvertently slapped a Royal Copley paper label on a piece normally designated Royal Windsor or Spaulding, it seems highly unlikely that the company would have allowed a permanent in-mold mark to remain if it cared at all about keeping its various lines separate and distinct. Estimated value: $10 each. *Carson Collection.*

This is the *Fish Vase,* 6 inches high and having three runners. It is not marked. This vase with gold decoration, along with one in gray, pink and blue can be seen on page 4. Estimated value: $35. *Carson Collection.*

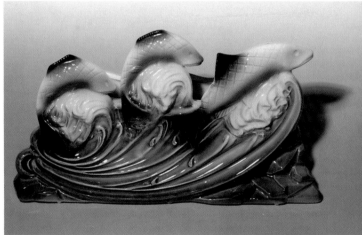

The *Jumping Salmon Planter* measures 8-1/2 x 11-1/8 inches. It is not marked, has three runners. It was also made in gray as shown by the Wolfes. Estimated value: as shown $85, gray $50. *Carson Collection.*

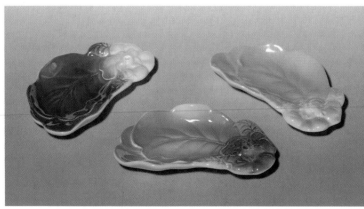

The *Cornucopia Vase* on the left stands 8 inches high. Note the Spaulding paper label just visible inside at top right. The one on the right is 8-1/8 inches high. Both have a gold stamp, Spaulding China / Pat. Pendg, on their bottoms. Estimated value: $15 each. *Carson Collection.*

These *Leafy Ashtrays* are 5 inches long, and have Royal Copley inkstamps. Estimated value: $5 each. *Carson Collection.*

These leaf ashtrays are larger than you might think, each measuring 7-1/2 inches in length. Mark is USA impressed. Estimated value: $5 each. *Carson Collection.*

This pair of leaf ashtrays are smaller than those above, measuring only 6-3/8 inches in length. Marks are the same. Estimated value: $5 each. *Carson Collection.*

This is the *Handled Leaf Creamer and Sugar.* The creamer is 3 inches high, the sugar 2-7/8 inches. Both are marked with Royal Copley in raised letters on the bottom. Estimated value: $25 per pair. *Carson Collection.*

Same heights and marks as above, different color. Estimated value: $25 per pair. *Carson Collection.*

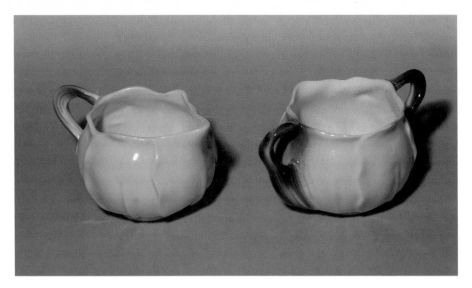

Again, same as above except for the color. Estimated value: $25 per pair. *Carson Collection.*

These unnamed lamps stand 10-1/4 inches high. The blue one is unmarked. Look closely and you will see a Spaulding paper label near the bottom of the green one. Estimated value: $35 each. *Carson Collection.*

This *Spaulding Rose Lamp*, 8-1/4 inches high, is unmarked. Estimated value: $35. *Carson Collection.*

The lamp base in the center is a repeat of above. The ones on the outside stand 8-1/4 inches high. None of the three is marked. Estimated value: center $35, outside $30 each. *Carson Collection.*

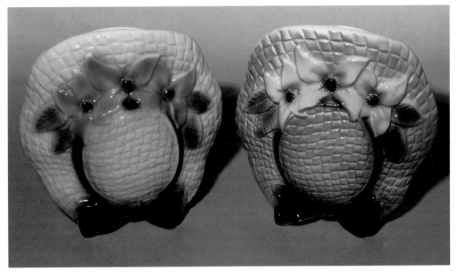

Although many of Spaulding China's items were used to decorate the kitchens of yesteryear, this *Big Apple Planter/ Wallpocket* is one of the few that was designed with a kitchen-specific theme. Height of this planter is 6 inches, it has two runners. It also has Royal Copley in raised letters, plus a Royal Copley paper label. Estimated value: $15. *Carson Collection.*

These are *Large Hat Planter/Wallpockets* 6 7/8" high, each marked Royal Copley in raised letters on the back. Estimated value: $25 each. *Carson Collection.*

The *Straw Hat with Bow Ashtray* measures 5-3/8 inches in diameter. Royal Copley appears in raised letters on its bottom. Estimated value: $5. *Osborne Collection.*

This *Small Hat Planter/Wallpocket* stands but 5-5/8 inches high. It carries the mark, Royal Copley, in raised letters on its back. Estimated value: $20. *Carson Collection.*

Small Hat Planter/Wallpockets in various color schemes, everything else same as above. Estimated value: $20 each. *Carson Collection.*

Two more *Straw Hat with Bow Ashtrays,* same as above except for the colors. Note that the one on the right has the same colors as the one shown above, but with the colors reversed. The same is true of the *Large Hat Planter/Wallpocket.* This is a common occurrence, not just with Spaulding but with other potteries, too. Reversing colors allowed a company to offer two different versions of the same product without any added expense. Estimated value: $5 each. *Carson Collection.*

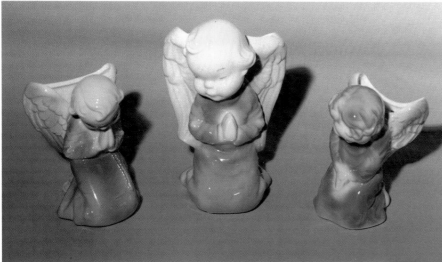

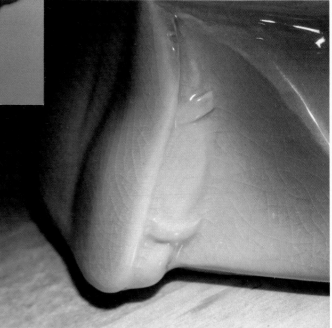

The angels in the center and at right are red versions of those shown in blue above. The one on the left, which is also called *Small Angel Planter,* is a whole different story. Its hands are held up under its chin instead of down in its lap, there is a cord on the front of its robe, and it is wearing sandals which are illustrated close up below. This one, along with the few others like it that have been reported, was made as a planter only, lacking the hole in back that would allow it to serve double duty as a wallpocket. It is 6-1/2 inches high and unmarked. Estimated value: left $75, center $30, right $25. *Carson Collection.*

Detail of the sandals on the *Small Angel Planter* on the left above. When searching for this planter, keep in mind that the main field identification feature would probably be the position of the hands. Don't be surprised if you find it in blue.

At left and right are the *Blackamoor Figurines.* That's the *Balinese Girl Planter* in the center. Is there a Balinese Boy Planter? It seems doubtful; to the best of my knowledge none has ever been reported. Although it does not appear as such because of the camera angle, all three of these pieces are the same height, 8-1/4 inches. All are unmarked, all have three runners. Estimated value: left and right $30 each, center $25. *Carson Collection.*

90

The *Blackamoor Planter/Wallpockets*. The one on the left stands 8-1/8 inches high, the one on the right 8-1/2 inches high. Each has Royal Copley in raised letters on the back. Estimated value: $40 each. *Carson Collection.*

Here is the *Blackamoor Prince Planter*. It is 8 inches high, has Royal Windsor in raised letters on the back. The back is flat but lacks the hole that would make it into a wallpocket, the same circumstance the Wolfes found with the one they photographed. Estimated value: $90. *Carson Collection.*

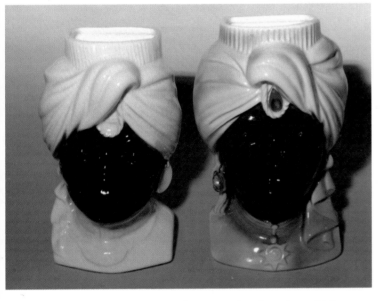

One in white, one with a plastic jewel and earring which may have been added after it left the factory. Estimated value: white $50, gray $40. *Carson Collection.*

The *Colonial Old Woman and Colonial Old Man Planter/wallpockets*, 8-1/8 and 8-1/4 inches high, respectively. They are marked by Royal Copley in raised letters on the back. Estimated value: $35 each. *Carson Collection.*

This is the *Dancing Lady Figurine.* Unmarked, it stands 8-1/4 inches high. Estimated value: $50. *Carson Collection.*

Two more *Dancing Lady Figurines,* both 8-1/4 inches high, both unmarked. Estimated value: $50 each. *Carson Collection.*

These *Dutch Girl and Boy with Bucket Planters* are just the type of things that bring folks into the hobby of collecting Spaulding. They are cute, well done, available and not very expensive. Heights average 6-3/8 inches. (I've seen some sets where the boy is slightly taller than the girl, others where the girl is slightly taller than the boy.) Unmarked, each of these planters has four runners. Estimated value: $15 each. *Carson Collection.*

Dutch Boy and Girl with Bucket Planters in red and blue, a less often seen color combination than blue and yellow. Estimated value: $20 each. *Carson Collection.*

Here is the boy with black, the girl with gold. Estimated value: boy $20, girl (with gold) $40. *Carson Collection.*

Now to the *Girl and Boy Leaning on Barrel Planters*, which generally run between 6-1/8 and 6-1/4 inches high. They are unmarked. Each has three runners. Estimated value: $15 each. *Carson Collection.*

Same kids, same buckets, different colors. Estimated value: $15 each. *Carson Collection.*

Barefoot Girl and Boy Planters. Both are 8 inches high, both are unmarked, both have three runners. Estimated value: $20 each. *Carson Collection.*

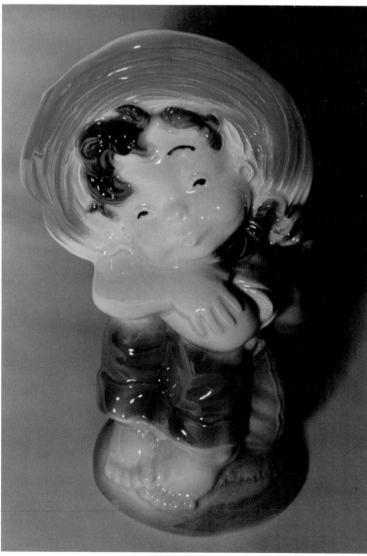

A *Barefoot Boy Planter* to match the girl above. Estimated value: $20. *Osborne Collection.*

Barefoot Girl and Boy Planters in two other color schemes. Estimated value: $20 each. *Carson Collection.*

These *Farmer Boy and Girl Planter/Wallpockets* stand 6-1/2 inches high. Each has three runners. Both have Royal Copley on the back in raised letters. Estimated value: $20 each. *Carson Collection.*

This *Farmer Boy and Girl* was made from a newer mold than the green and red pair, which makes more of a difference than one might think. Although we're talking only hundredths of an inch, the added detail makes for a much more natural looking figure, most noticeable here in the boy's rolled up shirt sleeve, the cuff of his overalls, not to mention the grain in the wood of the fence. Estimated value: $20 each. *Carson Collection.*

Here are the *Wide Brim Hat Boy and Girl Planter/Wallpockets*, each 8 inches high. Royal Copley is written in raised letters on the back of each one. Estimated value: $25 each. *Carson Collection.*

The wide brim kids in red and blue. Estimated value: $25 each. *Carson Collection.*

Pigtail Girl Planter/Wallpocket. It is 6-3/4 inches high, has two runners in addition to ©Royal Copley in raised letters on the back. Estimated value: $25. *Carson Collection.*

Red and aqua versions of the *Pigtail Girl.* Estimated value: $25 each. *Carson Collection.*

And gray and pink. Estimated value: $25 each. *Carson Collection.*

The *Girl and Wheelbarrow Planter,* 7 inches high, one runner, no mark. Estimated value: $15. *Carson Collection.*

The *Oriental Children with Big Vase Planters* stand 4-5/8 inches high. Each has two runners. They are not marked. Estimated value: $10 each. *Carson Collection.*

Everything the same but the colors. Estimated value: $10 each. *Carson Collection.*

More of the *Oriental Children with Big Vase Planters*. Estimated value: $10 each. *Carson Collection.*

The name of these is *Oriental Girl and Boy Planters*. They are 5-3/4 and 6-1/4 inches high, respectively. Mark is Royal Copley in raised letters on the back. Estimated value: $10 each. *Carson Collection*.

The *Oriental Girl and Boy Planters* in this combination of green, yellow and tan are the ones I seem to see most often. Estimated value: $10 each. *Carson Collection*.

This set with the blue-green is the one I see the least. Estimated value: $15 each. *Carson Collection*.

This pair, the *Oriental Boy and Girl with Large Basket on Back Planters*, are somewhat rarer than many of the other Oriental motif planters. The girl is 8 inches high, the boy 8-1/4 inches. Neither is marked, both have three runners. Estimated value: $20 each. *Carson Collection.*

Of the three sets shown, this one appears to be the color combination that is found the least. Estimated value: $15 each. *Carson Collection.*

Another long name for this pair, the *Oriental Girl and Boy with Basket on Ground Planters.* Heights are basically the same, 7-7/8 inches for her, 7-3/4 inches for him. Royal Copley is written in raised letters on the back. Estimated value: $10 each. *Carson Collection.*

Collectors like to refer to the female half of the basket-on-ground pair as the Copley pregnant girl, the reason why possibly showing up in this picture a bit better than in the other two. Estimated value: $10 each. *Carson Collection.*

These are the *Oriental Boy and Girl Figurines*, 8 and 7-3/4 inches high, respectively. They are not marked. Estimated value: $10 each. *Carson Collection*.

The boy at far right appears to have been sprayed with the same aqua glaze as the pair above but was given a thinner coat. Estimated value: $10 each. *Carson Collection*.

The *Clown Lamp* is quite a bit rarer than the *Clown Planter*. Size is somewhat different, 7-5/8 inches high. Note that it is actually a different piece of pottery than the planter, whereas the *Oriental Girl* lamp is simply an *Oriental Girl Figurine* attached to a metal base. Estimated value: clown $45, girl $25. *Carson Collection*.

The *Clown Planter* is 8-3/8 inches high, is unmarked but has two runners. Estimated value: $20. *Carson Collection*.

The big hat boy in red, unmarked. Another pair of these planters can be seen on page 5. Estimated value: $25. *Osborne Collection.*

The name of this piece is *Oriental Boy with Bamboo Side Planter*. It is 7-3/4 inches high, has three runners. Estimated value: $20. *Carson Collection.*

These are the *Chinese Boy and Girl with Big Hat Planter/ wallpockets*. They are marked ©Royal Copley in raised lettering on their backs. Each has two runners. Heights average 7-3/4 inches. Estimated value: $25 each. *Carson Collection.*

Here is a pair in a not only different, but also less common color scheme. This pair is not marked. Estimated value: $30 each. *Carson Collection.*

A pink one for a girl's room, a blue one for a boy's room. They are *Child Lamps*, each 7-3/4 inches high, unmarked. Estimated value: $30 each. *Carson Collection.*

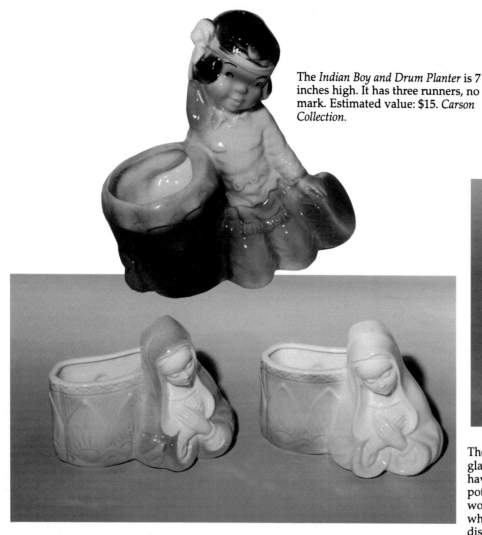

The *Indian Boy and Drum Planter* is 7 inches high. It has three runners, no mark. Estimated value: $15. *Carson Collection.*

Madonna Side Planters, 5-3/4 inches high. Both have Royal Windsor in raised lettering on the back. Estimated value: $15 each. *Carson Collection.*

The *Madonna Side Planter* with clear glaze. Some collectors and dealers I have talked to claim that pieces of pottery that are usually decorated are worth more money if they are pure white, because they are rarer. I strongly disagree, feeling anything that included additional work should be worth more than something that did not. Estimated value: $5. *Osborne Collection.*

There is no name differentiation in these two *Madonna Planters*. The taller one is 7-3/4 inches in height, the shorter one 6 inches. The larger piece has Royal Windsor in raised letters on the bottom while the smaller piece is unmarked. Estimated value: large $15, small $10. *Carson Collection.*

Same general height as above, same marks or lack of them. Estimated value: large $20, small $15. *Carson Collection.*

Large Madonna Planter in white. The small one was not available to photograph. Estimated value: large $10, small $5. *Carson Collection.*

Pirate Head Planter/Wallpockets. The one on the left is 8 inches high, the one on the right 8-1/4 inches. They are marked Royal Copley in raised lettering on the back. Estimated value: $50 each. *Carson Collection.*

These *Gloved Lady Planter/Wallpockets* are 6-1/2 inches high, have Royal Copley in raised letters on their backs. Estimated value: $30 each. *Carson Collection.*

Bare Shoulder Lady Planters, each 6 inches high. The one on the left has only a Royal Copley paper label, while the one on the right has Royal Copley impressed in its bottom. Estimated value: $20 each. *Carson Collection.*

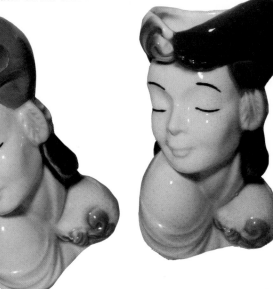

Everything the same as above except the addition of gold trim. Estimated value: $75. *Osborne Collection.*

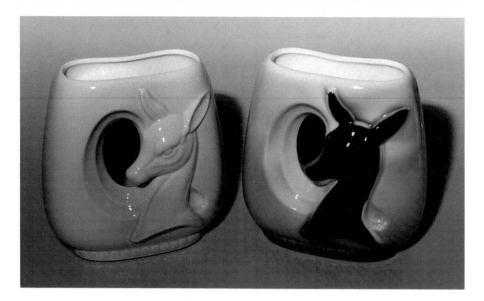

The *Deer Open Vase/Planter* stands 7-7/8 inches high, has two runners, is unmarked except by paper label. Estimated value: left $10, right $15. *Carson Collection.*

CHAPTER 8
THREE-DIMENSIONAL MOTIF

Based upon what you see at antique shows and flea markets, ivy may have been Spaulding's most popular nonfigural three-dimensional motif. The various ivy vases seem to show up everywhere. But from today's perspective, the several different fish vases would probably have be considered the real jewels. Look at the pictures and you get not only the impression that you could reach into the design and pick up the fish, but also that you would get your hand wet doing it.

This is the *Deer and Fawn Rectangular Planter.* It is 6-1/2 inches high. It has two runners, no mark. Note the Royal Copley paper label. Estimated value: $15. *Carson Collection.*

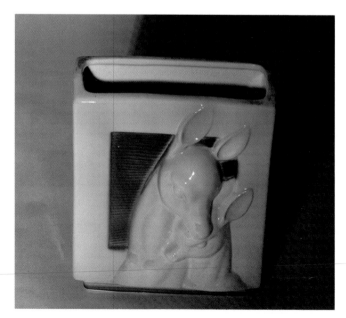

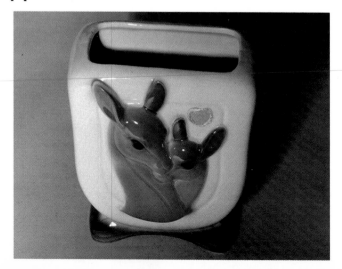

This piece, the *Deer and Doe Planter,* and the *Running Gazelles Planter* below, have horseshoe-shaped dry foots similar to those seen on products of the Brush Pottery, instead of the runners commonly used by Spaulding. Height is 7-1/2 inches. The planter is not marked. Estimated value: $10. *Carson Collection.*

The *Running Gazelles Planters* stand 6 inches high. They are not marked. Estimated value: left $25, right $10. *Carson Collection.*

The unmarked *Running Horse Planter* is 6 inches high, has two runners. Estimated value: $10. *Carson Collection.*

This *Grazing Horse Planter* is 4-5/8 inches high. It is unmarked, has two runners. Estimated value: $25. *Carson Collection.*

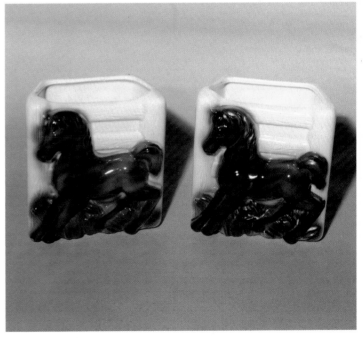

The *Pony Planter*, 5-1/4 inches high. The one on the left is unmarked. The one on the right, with antique gold, has Royal Copley in raised letters on the back. Estimated value: left $5, right $15. *Carson Collection.*

These are the *Bird in Flight Open Vase/Planters*. Each is 7-3/8 inches high. They have no permanent marks but do have two runners. Estimated value: left $35, right $15. *Carson Collection*.

Bunting Planter/Wallpockets, 5-1/4 inches high, marked on the back by the words Royal Copley in raised letters. Estimated value: $10 each. *Carson Collection*.

The *Rooster and Hen Plaque Planters* can stand free or hang on the wall. They are 6-5/8 inches high, have Royal Copley in raised letters on their backs. Estimated value: $20 each. *Carson Collection*.

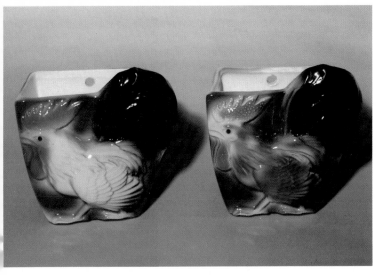

These are the *Walking Rooster Planter/Wallpockets,* 5-3/4 inches high with two runners on the bottom and Royal Copley in raised letters on the back. Like all Spaulding Pottery Company chickens, the white version carries a higher value. Estimated value: left $20, right $15. *Carson Collection.*

Spaulding made two *Cylindrical Fish Vases,* this one, at 7 inches, being the shorter. It has two runners, is unmarked. Estimated value: $10. *Carson Collection.*

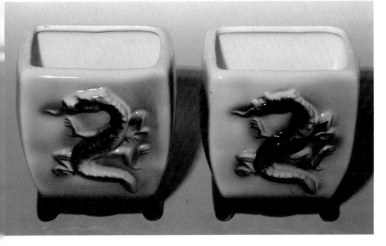

The *Oriental Style Footed Dragon Vases* are 5-1/4 inches high. They are not marked. Estimated value: $5 each. *Carson Collection.*

This baby ware mug is quite rare. It is 4-1/8 inches high, has two runners but no mark. Because it is babyware, be on the lookout for one in blue. Estimated value: $30. *Carson Collection.*

This taller *Cylindrical Fish Vase* has a height of 8-3/8 inches. Royal Copley appears in raised letters on the bottom. Estimated value: $10. *Carson Collection.*

The unnamed planter on the left stands 3-3/4 inches high, has three runners. The *Half Circle Fish Vase/Planter* on the right is 5-1/4 inches high. It also has three runners. Estimated value: $15 each. *Carson Collection.*

Height of this *Oriental Style Footed Fish Vase* is 5-3/8 inches. It is not marked. Estimated value: $10. *Carson Collection.*

These are the *Open Fish Vase/Planters*, 5-5/8 inches high with two runners. The one on the left has a Royal Copley paper label. One with gold decoration can be found on page 105. Estimated value: $15 each. *Carson Collection.*

Same size as above, different color. Estimated value: with heavy gold $25, without gold $10. *Carson Collection.*

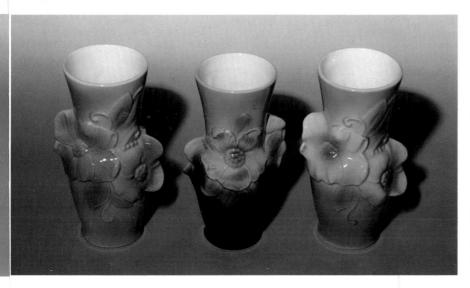

This picture shows two *Corsage Vases* from the front, one from the back. Estimated value: $10 each. *Carson Collection.*

Here's two from the back, one from the front. Estimated value: $10 each. *Carson Collection.*

Heights of all the *Carol's Corsage Vases* I measured ran between 7 and 7-1/8 inches. Each of them had a Royal Copley inkstamp. Estimated value: $10. *Carson Collection.*

This is called the *Floral Elegance Vase,* and maybe a few other choice names, too, as you often hear collectors tell stories about passing it by thinking it was a *Carol's Corsage Vase.* That is easy to do considering the similar motif and height, 7-7/8 inches. The vase on the left, shown from the front, has Royal Copley in raised letters on the bottom. The one on the right, shown from the back, carries a Royal Copley inkstamp. Estimated value: $10 each. *Carson Collection.*

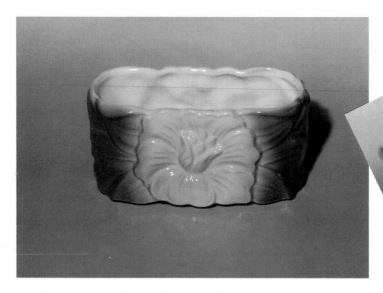

This is the *Big Blossom Planter,* 3 inches high, three runners, and a Royal Copley inkstamp. Estimated value: $5. *Carson Collection.*

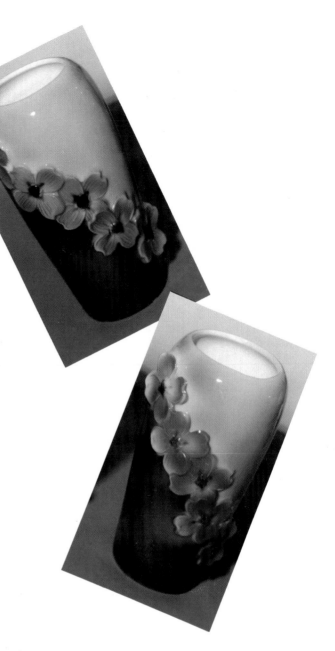

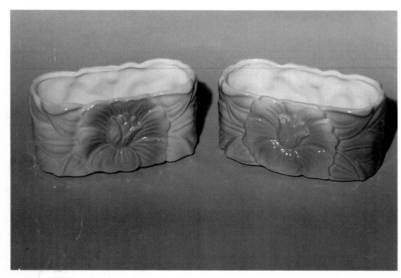

Two more *Big Blossom Planters.* Here again, as in so many cases, we view another example of reversed colors. Estimated value: $5 each. *Carson Collection.*

A pair of *Dogwood Vases,* one having light gold trim. They average 8 1/4" in height, Each has two runners, neither is marked. Estimated value: Plain $10, with gold $15. *Carson Collection.*

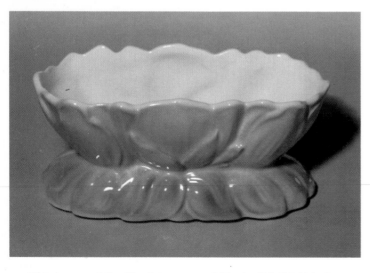

This is named the *Floral Arrangement Planter.* It is 3-1/4 inches high, has three runners on its bottom along with a Royal Copley inkstamp. Estimated value: $5.

That's the *Small Oval Dogwood Planter* on the left, 4-1/4 inches high with two runners. It is unmarked. On the right is the *Dogwood Oval Planter.* It's 3-3/4 inches high, has three runners, and is also unmarked. Estimated value: $5 each. *Carson Collection.*

On the left is the *Small Oval Bamboo Vase/planter,* 4-5/8 inches high, on the right the *Bamboo Oval Planter,* 5-5/8 inches. They have two runners and three runners, respectively. Estimated value: $5 each. *Carson Collection.*

Pome Fruit Pitchers, 7-7/8 inches high on the left, 8 inches high on the right. Each has a Royal Copley inkstamp. As you can see, both sides are shown. Estimated value: $15 each. *Carson Collection.*

The *Oval Bamboo Vase* shown here is shorter than the two similar pieces above. It stands only 3-3/4 inches high. The *Cylindrical Bamboo Vase* next to it towers at 8-1/2 inches. The shorter piece has three runners, the taller one two runners. Estimated value: left $5, right $10. *Carson Collection.*

Same pitchers as above but in other colors. Other marks, too, each having the words Royal Copley in raised letters on the bottom. Estimated value: $15 each. *Carson Collection.*

The *Fruit Plate Wall Plaque/Planter* is 7-1/8 inches high, has Royal Copley in raised letters on the back. Estimated value: $20. *Carson Collection.*

I guess we would call this a bamboo vase also, even though the pattern is quite different than that on the yellow and green pieces shown above. It stands 5 inches high, has two runners. Estimated value: $5. *Carson Collection.*

These are called *Harmony Vases*. They are 4-1/2 and 7-7/8 inches high. Each has two runners. Estimated value: left $5, right $10. *Carson Collection.*

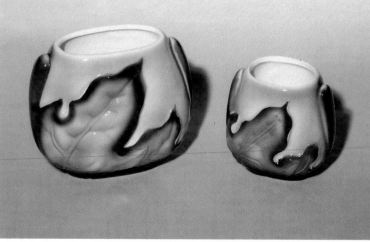

Heights of these *Harmony Vases* are 6-1/4 and 4-3/4 inches. Both have two runners. Estimated value: left $10, right $5. *Carson Collection.*

Harmony Vases in a different color scheme. Heights are 4-3/4 and 7-7/8 inches. Both have two runners. Estimated value: left $5, right $10. *Carson Collection.*

A gold-lined 4-3/4 inch *Harmony Vase.* Estimated value: $20. *Carson Collection.*

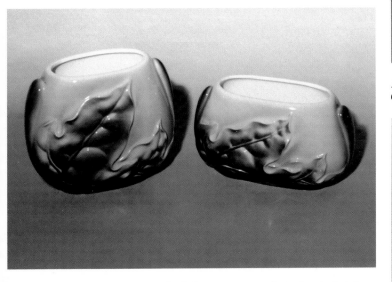

The *Harmony Vase* on the left measures 6-1/4 inches in height. The one on the right is 4-1/2 inches. Each has two runners. Estimated value: $5 each. *Carson Collection.*

Two *Black Floral Leaf and Stem Vases*, 4 and 6-7/8 inches high. Each has two runners. Be on the lookout for these vases with green instead of black flowers, as one has recently been discovered by an Ohio collector. Estimated value: $5 each. *Carson Collection.*

The pattern of this pair of vases is called *Stylized Leaf.* They are 5-3/4 and 8-1/4 inches high. The shorter one carries two runners, the larger one three. Estimated value: left $5, right $10. *Carson Collection.*

Two more *Trailing Leaf and Vine* items, the one on the left sporting gold trim. Heights are 4-7/8 and 8 inches; each has two runners. Estimated value: left $15, right $5. *Carson Collection.*

Stylized Leaf Vase with gold trim, 5-3/8 inches high with two runners. Estimated value: $20. *Carson Collection.*

On the left is a *Hardy Stem and Leaf Vase,* 7-1/4 inches high. It has two runners. The piece on the right is an 8-1/2 inch *Oval Homma Vase.* It also has two runners. Estimated value: $10 each. *Carson Collection.*

This *Trailing Leaf and Vine Vase* is 3-7/8 inches high. It has three runners. Estimated value: $5. *Carson Collection.*

This is a pair of *Laura's Twig Planters,* 5-1/8 inches high, Each has two runners. Although they appear very close in color, the one on the left is black, the one on the right green. Estimated value: $5 each. *Carson Collection.*

The 4-1/8 inch *Philodendron Footed Planter,* both with and without gold. Estimated value: Plain $5, with gold $15. *Carson Collection.*

Three green pieces. Left to right they are: 8-3/8 inch *Oval Homma Vase,* 4-1/4 inch *Round Triple Leaf Planter,* and 7-1/4 inch *Hardy Stem and Leaf Vase.* All have two runners. Estimated value: left to right $10, $5, $10. *Carson Collection.*

Here are the 7-1/8 and 8-1/8 inch *Ivy Footed Vases.* Estimated value: $10 each. *Carson Collection.*

A 3-7/8 *Philodendron Footed Planter* and 7-1/4 inch *Philodendron Footed Vase.* Estimated value: $5 each. *Carson Collection.*

Left to right, 4-1/2 inch *Ivy Footed Vase,* 4 inch *Ivy window box Planter,* 6-5/8 inch *Ivy Pillow Footed Vase.* Estimated value: left $5, middle $5, right $10. *Carson Collection.*

On the left is the 7-1/2 inch *Fall Arrangement Vase,* which has two runners. The Wolfes also called this pattern *Marine.* The piece on the right is the 5-3/4 inch *Fall Arrangement Planter.* Estimated value: left $10, right $5. *Carson Collection.*

The *Double Spray Planter* is 4-3/8 inches high. It has three
runners. Another example may be seen on page 17. Estimated
value: $5. *Carson Collection.*

The *Bow and Ribbon Ashtray* measures 5-3/4 x 4-3/4 inches and
has a raised Royal Copley on the bottom. Estimated value: $5.
Osborne Collection.

Two more *Bow and Ribbon Ashtrays,* same as above. Estimated
value: $5 each. *Carson Collection.*

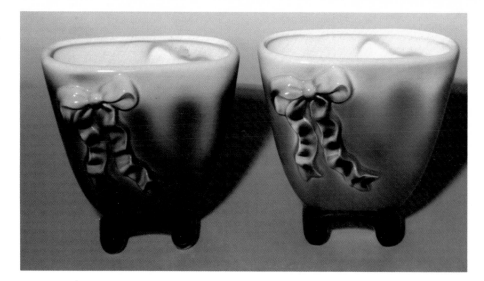

These *Footed Bow and Ribbon Vases* are 6-1/2 inches high. All that I have seen have been unmarked. Estimated value: $5 each. *Carson Collection.*

The *Large Round Riddle Planter,* on the left, stands 7 inches high. The *Oval Riddle Planter,* in the middle, is 4 inches, while the *Little Riddle Planter,* right, measures 4-7/8 inches. Estimated value: left $25, middle $15, right $10. *Carson Collection.*

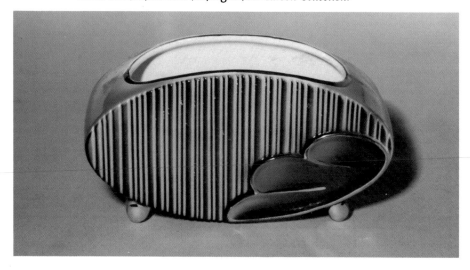

The *Oval Riddle Planter* with gold trim. It has a Shaffer gold inkstamp. Estimated value: $30. *Carson Collection.*

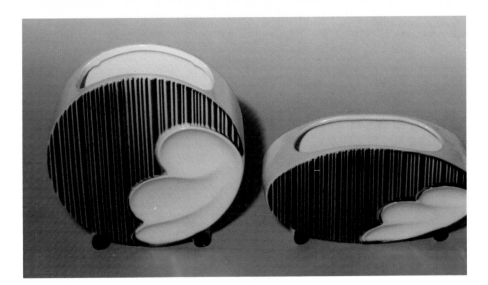

The *Large Round Riddle Planter* and the *Oval Riddle Planter* in black and white. Estimated value: left $25, right $15. *Carson Collection.*

The piece on the left is called the *Spooks Planter*. It is 4 inches high with three runners. The one on the right is the *Little Imagination Planter*, 4-1/8 inches high with two runners. Although they may not look it, both of these are decorated with green glaze. Estimated value: left $10, right $5. *Carson Collection.*

A black *Wilder Leaf Planter*, 4 inches high with two runners. Estimated value: $5. *Carson Collection.*

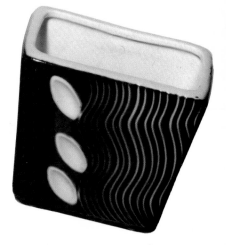

Here is the green version of the 4-1/8 inch *Three Tracks Planter*, which has two runners. Estimated value: $5. *Carson Collection.*

While this *Wilder Leaf Planter* may look the same as the one above, it's green instead of black. Estimated value: $5. *Osborne Collection.*

Royal Copley Ribbed Planters, 3-1/4, 4 and 5-1/8 inches high. Each has Royal / Copley on the bottom on two lines in raised letters. Estimated value: $5 each. *Carson Collection.*

Four more colors in which you may find the smallest *Ribbed Planter* above. Heights vary from 3-1/4 to 3-3/8 inches. Each sports Royal / Copley on two lines in raised lettering on the bottom. Estimated value: $5 each. *Carson Collection.*

The *Saltbox Planter/Wallpocket* stands 5-1/4 inches high, has Royal / Copley in raised letters on two lines on the back. Estimated value: $30. *Carson Collection.*

These vases were named *Mary Kay Planters* by the Wolfes. They are 6-1/4 inches high. Note that both are trimmed with gold. Appropriately, each has a gold stamp, Royal / Copley, on two lines. Estimated value: $10 each. *Carson Collection.*

CHAPTER 9
NON-THREE DIMENSIONAL MOTIF

The title of this chapter is somewhat of a misnomer. In the strictest sense of the word, some of the pieces shown below do have a three-dimensional motif. In all cases, however, it is very slight and represents only abstract design rather than recognizable objects.

In the neighborhood in which I grew up during the 1950s-- suburban, white middle class, lots of GI Bill and FHA housing mixed in with some pre-Depression construction--the type of pottery illustrated in this chapter was much more prevalent than that shown in any other chapter of the book.

A pair of gold lined vases. On the left is the *Floral Handle Vase*, 6-7/8 inches high. It is unmarked. The piece on the right is the *Blue Beauty Vase*, 6-1/4 inches. It is marked Royal / Copley in gold on two lines, plus a Royal Copley paper label. Estimated value: $10 each. *Carson Collection.*

A red version of the *Blue Beauty Vase,* same size as above, and sporting a Royal Copley paper label for all to see. The *Virginia Vase,* on the right, is 6-1/4 inches high, carries a Royal / Copley gold stamp on two lines. Estimated value: $10 each. *Carson Collection.*

An unnamed planter, 4-5/8 x 11-3/8 inches. Its mark, Royal / Windsor / USA, on three lines, is somewhat unusual in that the words Royal and Windsor are raised while USA is impressed. As you can see below, this piece was made in several different colors. Estimated value: $10. *Carson Collection.*

Same as above but in gray and pink. This one carried only the raised Royal Windsor for a mark, although it may be that the USA was undetectable due to a well used mold. Estimated value: $10. *Carson Collection.*

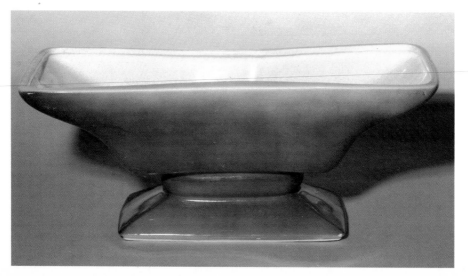

Approximately the same size again, 4-5/8 x 11-1/4 inches. This textured pebble glaze, as mentioned earlier, was applied by China Craft after the Spaulding plant closed. This piece has yet another variation of the same mark, Royal / Windsor / USA on three lines, all in raised letters. Estimated value: $10. *Carson Collection.*

This is a smaller version of the above planters measuring 4-1/4 x 8 inches. Mark is Royal / Windsor in raised letters on two lines, with USA impressed in another part of the bottom. Estimated value: $5. *Carson Collection.*

Now to the smallest known member of the above series. These measure 4-1/8 x 5-1/8 inches. Mark is Royal / Windsor in raised letters on two lines. Estimated value: $5 each. *Carson Collection.*

Same as above but with the China Craft pebble glaze. Estimated value: $5. *Carson Collection.*

These are called *Coma Vases.* Heights left to right are 5-1/8, 7-1/8 and 5-1/8 inches. All are unmarked, each has three runners. Estimated value: left and right $5 each, middle $10. *Carson Collection.*

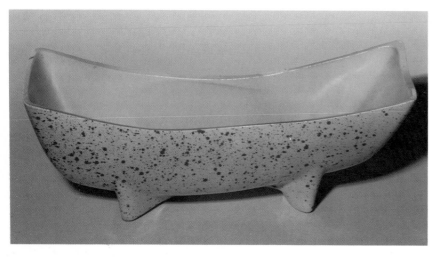

This is the *Boat-Shaped Planter,* 4 x 10-5/8 inches, and marked with an impressed USA. Estimated value: $5. *Carson Collection.*

Each of these vases is 6-5/8 inches high. Each has USA impressed on its bottom. Note the Royal Copley paper label on the one on the left. Estimated value: $5 each. *Carson Collection.*

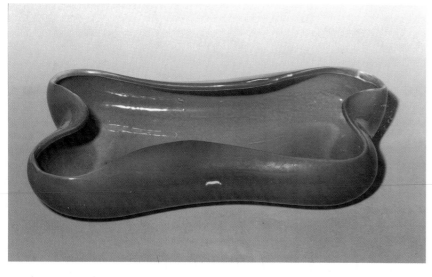

An unnamed planter, 13 inches long, marked Royal / Windsor on two lines in raised letters. Estimated value: $10. *Carson Collection.*

The vase on the right is the same as above, the one on the left was not measured. Both have USA impressed in their bottoms. Estimated value $5 each. *Carson Collection.*

This vase stands 6 inches high, has USA impressed. Estimated value: $5. *Carson Collection.*

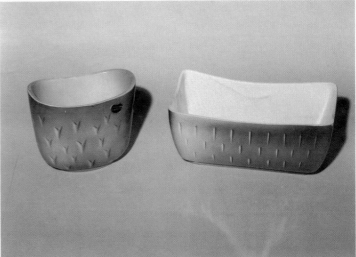

Now to the tracks pieces. On the left is a *Bird Tracks Planter,* 4-1/2 inches high, and carrying a Royal Copley paper label. The piece on the right, 3 1/2" high has some unnamed tracks that might best be described as long tracks. It is unmarked. Estimated value: $5 each. *Carson Collection.*

Similar to the above pink vase but taller and proportioned differently. Height is 7-7/8 inches, mark is, unsurprisingly, USA impressed. Estimated value: $10. *Carson Collection.*

This *Bird Tracks Planter* measures 3-1/4 x 8-3/8 inches. It is marked only by an impressed USA. Estimated value: $5. *Carson Collection.*

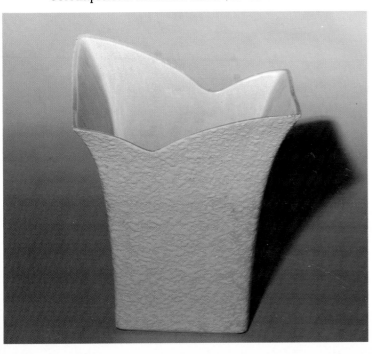

This is the *Royal Copley Vase,* 9 inches high, unmarked except for an impressed USA. The Wolfes, incidentally, showed this vase in a Spaulding glaze with a Royal Copley paper label. This one has a China Craft glaze. Estimated value: as shown $5, Spaulding glaze $10. *Carson Collection.*

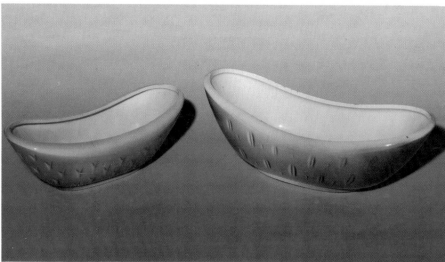

On the left is a *Bird Tracks Planter,* 3-1/4 x 8-3/8 inches, USA impressed. The larger *Strange Tracks Planter* on the right measures 3-1/4 x 10-5/8 inches. It is unmarked. Estimated value: $5 each. *Carson Collection.*

A 6-1/8 inch high *Bird Tracks Planter* that sports USA in raised letters on its bottom. Estimated value: $10. *Carson Collection.*

I lost the measurements of these candleholders with strange tracks. As I recall, they are about 5 inches high, maybe a hair shorter. Note the Royal Windsor paper labels. Estimated value: $10 per pair. *Courtesy of Ted and Lee Parent.*

The *Bird Tracks Planter* on the left is the same height as above, 6-1/8 inches, but in gray and pink instead of brown and yellow. The one on the right is 4-5/8 inches high. Marks were not recorded. Estimated value: left $10. right $5. *Carson Collection.*

This is a *Rib and Cornice Planter* measuring 3-1/2 x 7-1/2 inches. It is unmarked but carries three runners. Estimated value: $5. *Carson Collection.*

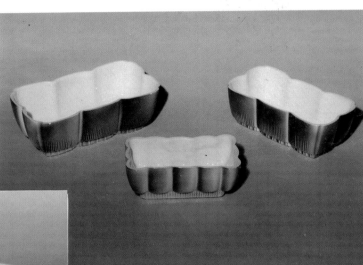

These are called *Sectioned Planters.* The one in front measures 2-1/2 x 6-1/4 inches. It is unmarked. The one at left rear is 2-3/4 x 8-5/8 inches, while the one at right rear is 2-5/8 x 7-5/8 inches. Each is marked Royal Copley on one line in raised letters. Estimated value: $5 each. *Carson Collection.*

Two smaller versions of the *Rib and Cornice Planter,* the one on the left being 3-3/8 x 5-3/8 inches, the one on the right 3-3/8 x 5 inches. Neither is marked, each has two runners. Estimated value: $5 each. *Carson Collection.*

Two examples of the *Parallel Rays Planter* line, these measuring 6 and 4-1/2 inches in height. Neither is marked. Estimated value: $5 each. *Carson Collection.*

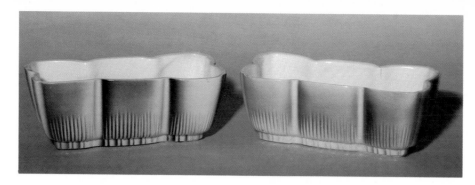

These Sectioned Planters are the same size as the smaller one above, 2-1/2 x 6-1/4 inches. Each is marked Royal Copley in raised letters on one line. Estimated value: $5 each. *Carson Collection.*

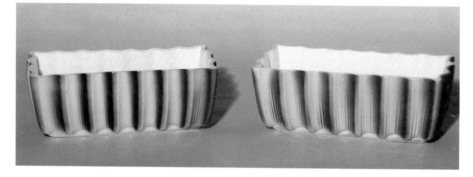

Here is a pair of *Hildegard Planters* measuring 2-3/8 x 6-3/8 inches. Neither is marked. Estimated value: $5 each. *Carson Collection.*

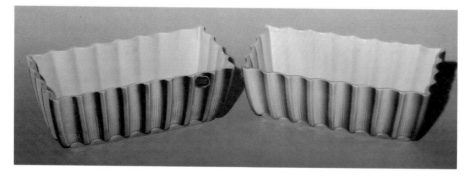

Two more *Hildegard Planters,* not only in different colors but also larger size, 2-7/8 x 8-1/2 inches. Note the Royal Copley paper label on the example on the left. Estimated value: $5 each. *Carson Collection.*

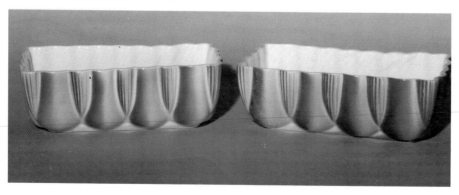

Similar to both the *Hildegard Planters* and the *Sectioned Planters* are the *Rex Planters,* 2-3/8 x 7-1/4 inches with Royal / Windsor in raised letters on two lines. Estimated value: $5 each. *Carson Collection.*

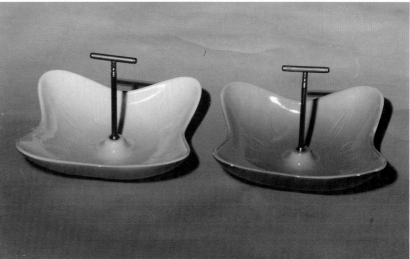

These unnamed candy dishes were made in several different shapes and sizes, this example being 9-1/8 inches across at its widest point. Its impressed mark reads USA / ® on two lines. Estimated value: $5 each. *Carson Collection.*

These are 7-1/8 inches square, with the same USA / ® impressed mark. Look closely and you will see they also have the molded design on the surface. Estimated value: $5 each. *Osborne Collection.*

This is the smaller size, 7-7/8 inches across at its widest point. It carries the same mark as above, USA / ® impressed on two lines. Spaulding candy dishes have also been found with ring handles instead of tee handles. Estimated value: $5 each. *Carson Collection.*

Measurements of this ashtray are 1-3/8 x 8-1/2 x 6-1/2 inches. Mark is USA impressed. Estimated value: $5. *Osborne Collection.*

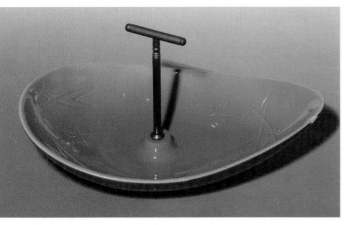

Note the addition of the molded design on the surface of this 9-1/8 inch model. Like the others, it is marked with an impressed USA / ® on two lines. Estimated value $5. *Carson Collection.*

On the left is a *Strange Tracks Ashtray*, on the right a *Bird Tracks Ashtray*, although neither's tracks, which are on the outside, show up very well in the picture. Each is 2 inches high, each is marked USA by impression. Estimated value: $5 each. *Osborne Collection.*

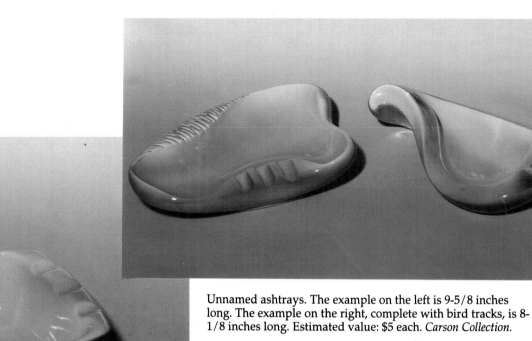

Unnamed ashtrays. The example on the left is 9-5/8 inches long. The example on the right, complete with bird tracks, is 8-1/8 inches long. Estimated value: $5 each. *Carson Collection.*

A *Strange Tracks Ashtray,* 5-1/2 inches across. Impressed mark is USA. Estimated value: $5. *Carson Collection.*

This unmarked ashtray is 7-3/4 inches long. Estimated value: $5. *Carson Collection.*

The ashtray on the left, same as above, has a length of 7-3/8 inches while the one on the right measures 9-3/8 inches. Both are unmarked. Estimated value: $5 each. *Carson Collection.*

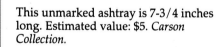

More ashtrays, both measuring 8-1/2 inches in length. Neither is marked. Estimated value: $5 each. *Carson Collection.*

A *Plain Jane Planter*, 3-3/8 inches high. A look at its bottom would reveal Royal / Copley in raised letters on two lines. Estimated value: $5. *Carson Collection.*

At the present time the origin of the decorative accessory holding this pair of *Plain Jane Planters* is unknown. It may have been purchased by Spaulding from a metals manufacturing concern. Or a metals manufacturing concern may have purchased planters from Spaulding to place in its own products. A third possibility would be that Spaulding may have experimented with making accessory pieces for its pottery for a short while. Although I have never heard that suggested, it was not unknown in the pottery industry. The subject of my last book, Ceramic Arts Studio, developed a secondary business, Metal Arts Studio, for exactly that purpose. And, of course, there is a fourth possibility. That would be that it's completely unrelated to Spaulding, perhaps some nameless owner of the pair of planters discovering that a metal rack that had been lying around the garage or basement for years was quite suitable to hold the *Plain Janes*. Estimated value: undetermined. *Carson Collection.*

135

Spaulding *Coasters* measure 4-1/2 inches in diameter. Sometimes they carry a Royal Windsor mark, other times they are unmarked. Some have been seen with Royal Copley paper labels. According to the Wolfes, Spaulding had the *Coasters* made by a company called Gem, which was also in Sebring. Starting at top left and going clockwise, the cars illustrated are an 1898 Winton, 1896 Ford, 1895 Duryea and 1877 Felden. Estimated value: $15 each. *Carson Collection.*

Chapter 10
Decal Ware

Decal ware was apparently one of the first things made at Spaulding, and also one of the first to go. According to most accounts, the company ceased making it in 1947. From our 1994 vantage point we may reasonably assume production ended for one of three reasons. The company may have wished to avoid products that required an extra firing. Technical difficulties may have resulted in too much scrap which would have made the cost noncompetitive. Or it may simply not have sold well. For whatever reason or combination of reasons, its short production run is reflected in its relative rarity today, but strangely, not necessarily in its market value.

The Most troublesome aspect of decal ware is identifying unmarked lamps, several of which are shown at the end of this chapter. The problem is that while all of them have characteristics of Spaulding's marked lamps, very similar pieces made by numerous potteries abound in the 1940s and 1950s. Unfortunately, that means positive identification is virtually impossible until like items are found bearing either Spaulding China Company paper labels or permanent marks.

Again, clockwise from top left, 1902 Autocar Runabout, 1899 Packard, 1902 Autocar Runabout (different color) and 1903 Cadillac. Estimated value: $15 each. *Carson Collection.*

These *Coasters* are the same size as above but have decals of paintings instead of cars. Estimated value: $15 each. *Carson Collection.*

While this may appear to be a plate because of the way I photographed it, it is actually a *Royal Copley Plaque Planter/ Wallpocket,* 8-1/4 inches in diameter. Like many Spaulding wallpockets, this one was designed so it could also function as a freestanding, though precariously thin, planter. Estimated value: $20. *Carson Collection.*

More decals of paintings. Estimated value: $15 each. *Carson Collection.*

All four of the wallpockets shown in this chapter have Royal / Copley in raised letters on two lines on their backs. Estimated value: $20. *Carson Collection.*

Sometimes the variety of decals on *Coasters* seems almost endless. There is little doubt that new examples will be cropping up for years. Estimated value: $15 each. *Osborne Collection.*

Because of the angle from which these pictures were shot, the wallpocket/planters appear to be slightly elliptical. Actually they are perfectly round. Estimated value: $20. *Carson Collection.*

This babyware vase is 6-3/8 inches high. Unmarked, it is a very very light blue. Estimated value: $15. *Carson Collection.*

The Wolfes showed one of these with just the green border, no decal. Another has been found recently with The Lord's Prayer on it. Estimated value: $20. *Carson Collection.*

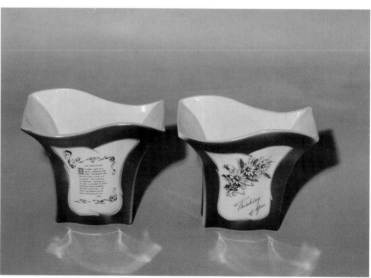

These are the same size as above. The one on the left is marked USA with a gold stamp. The one on the right is unmarked. Estimated value: $10 each. *Carson Collection.*

Two decal vases, one for an anniversary, the other a birthday. Height of each is 6-1/4 inches, neither is marked. Estimated value: $10 each. *Carson Collection.*

Cylindrical vases, each 8-1/4 inches high. They are unmarked. Estimated value: $15 each. *Carson Collection.*

The *Decal Pitchers* are each 6-1/8 inches high, the *Decal Vase* 6-1/4 inches. All three have Royal Copley stamped in gold on their bottoms. Estimated value: $5 each. *Carson Collection.*

Here again we run into Spaulding's green and black which are often difficult to tell apart. The ones on the outside are green, the one on the inside is black. Heights are 8-1/8 inches for the green examples, 8-1/4 inches for the black one. Estimated value: $10 each. *Carson Collection.*

Each of these *Decal Pitchers* is 6-1/8 inches high. Each has a Royal Copley gold stamp. Estimated value: $5 each. *Carson Collection.*

This is the reverse of the above picture, black on the outside, green on the inside. All three are 8-1/4 inches high, all three are unmarked. Estimated value: $10 each. *Carson Collection.*

Height of these *Decal Vases* is 7 inches. The one on the right carries a Royal Copley paper label, the others are unmarked. Estimated value: $10 each. *Carson Collection.*

As above but in butterscotch. Estimated value: $10. *Osborne Collection.*

Butterscotch Decal Vases. The example in the middle, which is being shown from the back, stands 6-1/4 iches high, and has a Royal Copley gold stamp. The other two are 6-1/8 inches high, and each has a gold stamp reading Pat. Reg. on its bottom. Estimated value: $10 each. *Carson Collection.*

Heights here, left to right, are 8-1/4 and 8-3/8 inches. Both vases are marked, Spaulding China / Pat. Pending, on two lines in gold. Estimated value: $10 each. *Osborne Collection.*

Here is a pair of taller Decal Vases, 10-1/4 inches on the left, 10 inches on the right. Marks were not recorded. Estimated value: left $15, right $10. *Osborne Collection.*

This vase stands 8 inches high, has a very identifiable Royal Copley gold stamp. Estimated value: $10. *Osborne Collection.*

A pair of identical vases but with different decals. Height is 4-1/8 inches. While the piece on the right is unmarked, the one on the left has a Royal Copley gold stamp. Estimated value: $5 each. *Carson Collection.*

These vases are also 4-1/8 inches high. Both have Royal Copley gold stamps. Estimated value: $5 each. *Carson Collection.*

Each of these vases is 6-1/4 inches high. Each has a Royal Copley gold stamp. Note that the one on the right is like one shown in butterscotch above. Estimated value: $5 each. *Carson Collection.*

The pottery part of both of these lamps measures 7-7/8 inches in height. The one on the left has a Spaulding paper label, the one on the right is unmarked. Estimated value: left $15, right not determined. *Carson Collection.*

Neither of these lamps is marked, but both appear to be Spaulding. Heights are 7-7/8 inches on the left, 8 inches on the right. Estimated value: not determined. *Carson Collection.*

This homemade contraption started out as a simple lamp, then was apparently improved upon by some do-it-yourselfer who could not find enough other projects to keep him busy and added a 7-inch ivory Fiesta plate for a base. The plate made it impossible to tell whether or not it is marked. Estimated value: not determined. *Carson Collection.*

The lamp on the left was apparently made by a consumer as it is simply a vase filled with plaster with a pipe nipple running down through it. It is 8 inches high and has a Royal Copley inkstamp. The one on the right, a real lamp, is unmarked, 8-1/8 inches high. Estimated value: not determined. *Carson Collection.*

The bottom of this two-piece model is 5-3/8 inches high, the top 6 inches. It is not known if it is marked. Estimated value: not determined. *Carson Collection.*

This lamp stands 11 inches high, is unmarked. Estimated value: not determined. *Carson Collection.*

══════BIBLIOGRAPHY══════

Brink, Helen, "Royal Copley," *American Clay Exchange*, volume 4 number 3, El Cajon, California, March 1984.

Derwich, Jenny B. and Latos, Dr. Mary, *Dictionary Guide to United States Pottery and Porcelain (19th and 20th Century)*, Jenstan, Franklin, Michigan, 1984.

Huxford, Sharon and Bob, *Schroeder's Antiques Price Guide*, 1993 and 1994 editions, Collector Books, Paducah, Kentucky.

Kovel, Ralph and Terry, *Kovel's Antiques & Collectibles Price List*, 1993 and 1994 editions, Crown Publishers, Inc., New York.

Lehner, Lois, *Lehner's Encyclopedia of U.S. Marks on Pottery, Porcelain & Clay*, Collector Books, Paducah, Kentucky, 1988.

Posgay, Mike, and Warner, Ian, *The World of Head Vase Planters*, Antique Publications, Marietta, Ohio, 1992.

Schneider, Mike, *Animal Figures*, Schiffer Publishing Ltd., West Chester, Pennsylvania, 1990.

-----"Royal Copley: forget the dime-store image," *Antique Week*, volume 23 number 36, Knightstown, Indiana, December 3, 1990.

Wolfe, Leslie C. and Marjorie A., copyright by Joseph M. Devine, *More About Royal Copley Plus Royal Windsor and Spaulding*, Collector Books, Paducah, Kentucky, 1992

-----*Royal Copley Plus Royal Windsor and Spaulding*, Collector Books, Paducah, Kentucky, 1992.

Top Value Stamps Family Gift Catalog, Top Value Enterprises, Inc., Dayton, Ohio, 1972.

OTHER BOOKS BY MIKE SCHNEIDER FROM.....
SCHIFFER PUBLISHING

Majolica Mike Schneider. A comprehensive look at this soft-bodied, brightly colored pottery with its high-relief decoration and clear lead glaze. The book is amply illustrated with color photographs, and the various forms that Majolica took are covered in detail. Included are pitchers, platters, plates, leaf plates, syrups, cigarette holders, ashtrays, humidors, and other forms. Price guide included.
Size: 6" x 9"   170 color photos   144 pp.
ISBN: 0-88740-228-3   soft cover $14.95

Animal Figures Mike Schneider. An exploration of the popular field of collecting animal images. Figures are organized by firm and species. Included, too, are carnival chalkware, characters such as Mickey Mouse, and useful animal figures such as bottle openers and banks. Includes price guide.
Size: 8 1/2" x 11"   1029 photos   256 pp.
ISBN: 0-88740-275-5   softcover $29.95

The Complete Cookie Jar Book Mike Schneider. More than 2000 color photographs present a visual and textual history of this unique kitchen art form. The only book to record the heights of jars and to offer photographic images of marks, Country Folk   Art Magazine says "this is one of the best books on the subject." Includes price guide.
Size: 9" x 12"   2000+ color photos   300 pp.
ISBN:0-88740-336-0   hard cover $59.95

Stangl and Pennsbury Birds: Identification and Price Guide Mike Schneider. In this first book of its kind, Schneider shows the entire Stangl Birds of America series, 60 examples of Pennsbury birds, and the little known but desirable Stangl animal figures in beautiful color photos. This user-friendly book, lists the Stangl birds by model number, and includes an alphabetical name index for complete and easy cross referencing. Close-up photos of marks and a price guide make this beautiful volume invaluable for collectors and dealers.
Size: 6" x 9"   209 color photos Price Guide/Index
160 pp. ISBN: 0-88740-612-2   hard cover $19.95

The Complete Salt and Pepper Shaker Book Mike Schneider. The largest, most comprehensive and colorful guide to salt and pepper shakers ever published shows more than 1600 sets of figural shakers in full color including some that have never appeared in a book before. Company histories, measurements of shakers, and pictures of marks and paper labels are among the book's innovative features. This book is a must for collectors, dealers, and appraisers.
Size: 9" x 12"   Price Guide   252 pp.
ISBN: 0-88740-494-4   hardcover $49.95

Ceramic Arts Studio: Identification and Price Guide Mike Schneider. From 1942 to 1955, this Wisconsin pottery focused on the production of slipcast figurines which are avidly collected today. Mike Schneider captures the beauty and charm of these figurines, providing a reference that has long been needed by collectors. The photographs are accompanied by a wealth of useful information including the history of the company and hints on care, repair, preservation, valuing, fakes and reproductions.
Size: 8 1/2" x 11"   267 color photos Price Guide   112 pp.
ISBN: 0-88740-604-1   hard cover $24.95